PLAYED IN GERMANY

A FOOTBALLING JOURNEY THROUGH A NATION'S SOUL

KIT HOLDEN

DUCKWORTH

First published in the United Kingdom by Duckworth in 2024

Duckworth, an imprint of Duckworth Books Ltd
1 Golden Court, Richmond, TW9 1EU, United Kingdom
www.duckworthbooks.co.uk

For bulk and special sales please contact
info@duckworthbooks.com

© Kit Holden, 2024

All rights reserved. No part of this publication may be reproduced, stored in a retrieval system, or transmitted, in any form or by any means electronic, mechanical, photocopying, recording or otherwise, without the prior permission of the publisher.

The right of Kit Holden to be identified as the Author of this Work has been asserted by him in accordance with the Copyright, Designs and Patents Act 1988.

A catalogue record for this book is available from the British Library.

Book design and typesetting by Danny Lyle

Printed and bound in Great Britain by Clays Ltd, Elcograf S.p.A.

Paperback ISBN: 978-0-7156-5541-2
eISBN: 978-0-7156-5542-9

'A fascinating perspective not just on German football but on Germany itself. Immaculately researched and entertainingly written, Holden combines an evident affection for his subject with the clear judgement to critique it fairly' **Jonathan Liew, *Guardian***

'Kit Holden has travelled across this enchanting, diverse and often misunderstood country to explain in vivid detail the unbreakable bond it has with the "Beautiful Game"' **John Kampfner, bestselling author of *Why the Germans Do it Better***

'This is among the very finest books written about German football. In fact, to call it a sports book is to do it a disservice, such is the breadth of its coverage and the scope of its analysis of the country's history and culture. A tremendous accomplishment and a terrific read' **Sebastian Stafford-Bloor, *The Athletic***

'Absolutely wunderbar! Kit Holden's book is remarkably enlightening about both German football and society. It's indispensable for anyone who wants to discover more about one of the continent's great football cultures' **Adrian Goldberg**

'A great guide to Germany's football heartlands, Kit Holden wisely places the culture of the game in the contexts of the society around it: local and international, traditional and modern, political and personal. *Played in Germany* is a cracking read – fascinating and informative' **Michael Wagg, author of *The Turning Season: DDR-Oberliga Revisited***

'This engaging and insightful book is a perfect illustration of how events on and off the pitch have given each German club a special character and identity' **Kevin Hatchard, Bundesliga World Feed TV Commentator**

Also by Kit Holden

Scheisse! We're Going Up!

For Josie

Author's Note

Some of the cultural and historical regions talked about in this book are, by definition, contested and difficult to define on a modern map of Germany. In these cases, I have attempted to portray the regions as a modern German would be likely to understand them, especially in the context of football. I apologise to anyone who feels the maps misrepresent their cultural identity.

CONTENTS

Prologue - **Germany?** ... ix

1. **Leipzig: A Land of Two Halves** ... 1
2. **The Rhineland: Jesters and Kings** ... 31
3. **The Ruhr: Heart and Coal** ... 61
4. **Stuttgart: Made in Swabia** ... 89
5. **Frankfurt: Nation Building** ... 113
6. **Hamburg: Political Football** ... 143
7. **Munich: Laptops and Lederhosen** ... 169
8. **Berlin: Turning Point** ... 195

Epilogue - **Euro** ... 221

Acknowledgements ... 227
List of Illustrations ... 229
Endnotes ... 231
Bibliography ... 233

MODERN GERMANY

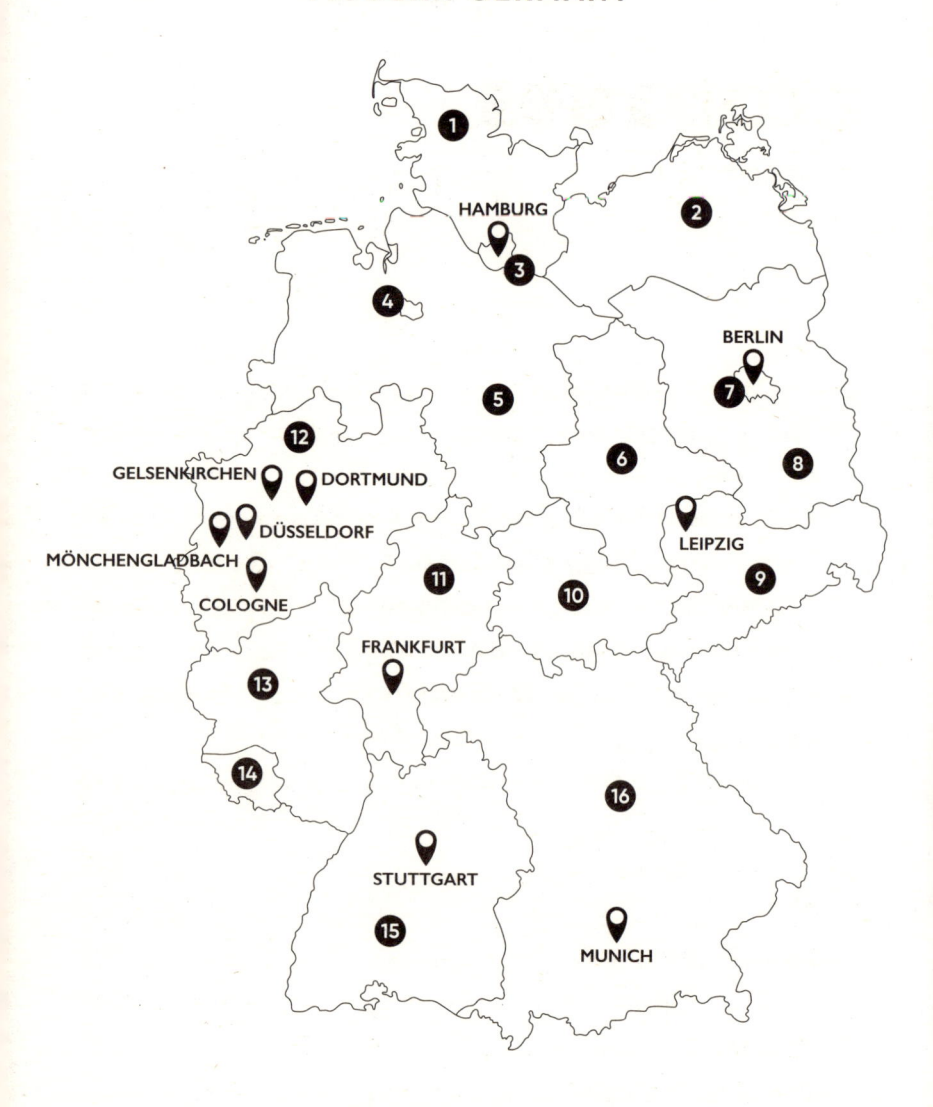

Federal states of Germany

1. Schleswig-Holstein
2. Mecklenburg-Vorpommern
3. Hamburg
4. Bremen
5. Lower Saxony
6. Saxony-Anhalt
7. Berlin
8. Brandenburg
9. Saxony
10. Thuringia
11. Hesse
12. North Rhine-Westphalia
13. Rhineland-Palatinate
14. Saarland
15. Baden-Württemberg
16. Bavaria

PROLOGUE
GERMANY?

Close your eyes and imagine a stereotypical German. What do you see? A man in lederhosen, perhaps, or a woman in a dirndl. Maybe they are on their way to Oktoberfest, a litre-glass of beer in one hand and a sausage in the other. Or perhaps you prefer a different cliché: a high-flying businessperson, a stern manager type behind the wheel of a German-made car like a BMW or an Audi. If you are a football fan you might see one of the great German players: Franz Beckenbauer, Lothar Matthäus or Thomas Müller.

By this point, anyone who is not from Bavaria will be getting a little hot under the collar. All of the above, from the beer festival to BMW and Beckenbauer, are actually Bavarian. And while all Bavarians are, by definition, German, most Germans emphatically do not consider themselves Bavarian. In fact, not even all Bavarians consider themselves entirely Bavarian, but that is a story for a later chapter.

The point is that when the rest of the world reaches for a German cliché, they tend to find one in Bavaria. And to a certain extent, that is understandable. Bavaria is Germany's largest state by area and home to some of its biggest companies and cultural exports, including its thirty-three-time football champions Bayern Munich. It is the most obvious image that most people around the globe have of Germany, and it is often the face that Germany is happy to show the world. It is no coincidence that the opening game of Euro 2024 will take place in Munich.

Yet Bavaria is not quintessentially German, any more than haggis, bagpipes and Burns Night are quintessentially British. In reality, it is extremely difficult to pin down anywhere that is typically German. This is a country that stretches from the Alps to the North Sea, a place that borders Belgium and France but which is also only a six-hour drive from Ukraine and Belarus. In total, it shares a border with nine different countries, and most of those frontiers have shifted back and forth as the idea of Germany has changed over the centuries. In the last two hundred years alone, the country has taken at least eight distinct forms, from a loose collection of autonomous kingdoms to a murderous, fascist dictatorship hell-bent on conquering the rest of Europe. Thankfully, it is now a modern, peaceful democracy. Yet even thirty-five years ago, it was still divided into two states on opposite sides of the Cold War.

Germany, in other words, is complicated, and when thousands of fans descend on the country for Euro 2024, they will quickly find out that no two German places are the same. Even modern Germany is still a country made up of small countries: a Federal Republic consisting of sixteen individual states, each with their own regional government. Berlin may be the capital, but in reality Germany has several different centres of gravity: Frankfurt is the financial centre; the powerful manufacturing base is in southern cities like Stuttgart and Munich; Hamburg, in the north, is responsible for shipping German goods across the world.

As anyone in any of these places will tell you, they all have their distinct regional cultures, with different dialects, different food and different traditions. All Germans speak German, but a Bavarian will struggle to understand Plattdeutsch, the dialect spoken in the far north. Similarly, most Germans really do love beer and sausages, but they also fiercely disagree on who makes them best. Many of these disputes have centuries-old roots, and yet they are also a fundamental part of Germany's modern self-image. National pride, after all, is still a thorny issue in this country. Less than a century after German nationalism unleashed the Second World War and committed a brutal genocide against Europe's Jewish population, many Germans would still feel queasy describing themselves as patriots. Yet most are still proud to be Berliners, Bavarians, Hessians or Hanseatics.

So what *does* bind all these people together, beyond their dark past, their love of beer and their shared citizenship? One answer, at least, is football.

Football is everywhere in Germany. Almost every major city has at least one grand old club, and almost every region has a fiercely contested rivalry. In terms of popularity, it dwarfs all other sports, and since the country hosted the World Cup in 2006, it has taken up an ever bigger share of the cultural landscape. More than seven million people in Germany are registered members of a football club, almost a tenth of the entire population. If you want to know how Germans tick, football is as good a window to look in at as any. It offers an insight not only into the local and regional diversity, but also the economy and history of the country at large. Many of Germany's top-flight clubs have close relationships with German business giants such as Bayer and Volkswagen, while the history of German football is also the history of a changing country. Germany's first World Cup win, in 1954, was a huge cultural moment in the country's recovery from the moral depths of the Nazi era. Its third, in 1990, came just a few months before the reunification of East and West Germany.

Germany has not always been the sexiest of the big football nations. The Germans have neither the charisma of the Brazilians, nor the aestheticism of the Spanish and the Dutch. They don't even have the fatalistic sense of tragedy and redemption that seems to underpin the football psyches of England, Italy or Argentina. As four-time World Cup winners, they certainly don't have the plucky charm of the underdog. In the famous words of Gary Lineker: 'Football is a simple game. Twenty-two men chase a ball for ninety minutes and at the end, the Germans always win.' For many both inside and outside the country, the famous 'winning mentality' is the defining trait of German football culture. Ahead of Euro 2024, with the national team at one of its lowest ebbs for decades, there are many proclaiming the end of the German game.

Yet for me at least, this idea has never rung entirely true. My own love of German football began with a defeat: as a five-year-old child in a Bayern Munich shirt crying bitter tears as Manchester United won the Champions League final in injury time in 1999. Like most defeats, it proved a lot more formative than victory, and a quarter of a century later I find myself writing about German football for a living. For this book, I have travelled to stadiums across the country, from Stuttgart to Berlin and from Hamburg to Munich. If there is one constant in all of them, it is that winning isn't everything.

Nowadays, German football is known as much for its vibrant fan culture as for what happens on the pitch. Compared to other major European countries, this is a place where ticket prices remain low and high-level football remains accessible. In Germany, you can see a Bundesliga game for fourteen euros, a

Champions League game for twenty-five euros, and buy a season ticket at Bayern Munich for 165 euros. Fans are treated like adults, trusted to drink alcohol in the stadiums, and watch the game standing up in a safe and responsible way. They respond by delivering some of the best atmospheres in Europe. When Italian World Cup winner Leonardo Bonucci moved to Union Berlin in 2023, he was amazed to find the fans stayed for fifteen minutes after the game to celebrate the team, even after a listless 2–0 defeat to Hoffenheim: 'When I got home, my son turned to me and said: "Papa, why were they cheering you when you lost?"'

As football has become more and more commercialised, German fan culture has also become a beacon for those trying to reclaim the game in other countries. Here, as elsewhere, football clubs operate like big businesses, yet unlike in England, they are not private companies. German fans can also become members of their clubs, giving them the right to vote at board elections and attend the annual general meeting. In the late 1990s, as more and more football clubs began to open up to private investors, German football introduced the 50+1 rule to ensure that the members retained majority control. In a world where football has increasingly become a plaything for corporations and nation states, the German game has managed to retain some small traces of people power. In Germany, a football fan is not just a fan or a consumer. They are part of a community.

Which is why the real soul of German football is not to be found in the fortunes of the national team, but on the terraces of club football. It is in club football where the country's local and regional identities are played out, where German fans articulate what they want from the game, and where you find out most about Germany and the Germans.

That, in a nutshell, is the idea behind this book. It is a football book, but it is mainly concerned with what football has to say about the history, culture and politics of Germany and its various regions. It is a work of journalism rather than serious academic research, and it is based on interviews with German football fans of all shapes and sizes, from World Cup winners and leading politicians to musicians, goat-herds, historians and beer brewers.

Because Germany is a country of many countries, this book too is a mosaic. Each chapter is a portrait of a different host city of Euro 2024. Where – as in the case of the Ruhr or the Rhineland – two cities belong to the same region and cultural tradition, I have put them together in a single chapter. Likewise, the chapters on individual cities are often not just about the towns themselves, but also their broader region and culture and their place in the national conversation. Taken as a whole, the eight chapters should build a portrait of Germany as it is in the early 2020s, and the story of how it got to be there.

In Germany, as everywhere else in the world, events are now moving with astonishing speed, and there are some topics that are therefore beyond the scope of this book. The Hamas terrorist attacks of 7 October 2023 and the subsequent Israeli invasion of Gaza had huge implications for German society, yet most of the interviews I conducted were carried out before the conflict erupted, so I have treated the issue with a light touch. Likewise, every word in this book was written before the end of the 2023/24 football season. The state of geopolitics, the situation in Germany and the power dynamics of the Bundesliga may all look dramatically different by the time you, the reader, pick up this book. The account of Germany in these pages does not

PROLOGUE

profess to be predictive, definitive or comprehensive. But it is, hopefully, enlightening.

Unlike Euro 2024, and in defiance of the clichés, the story does not begin in Munich and Bavaria. It begins in the city where German football was officially founded, and which played a huge role in the creation of the modern German state. A place on the frontline of the battle for fan power, where football is often cast as a matter of life, death and morality. It begins in Leipzig.

DIVIDED GERMANY, 1945–1990

1
LEIPZIG
A LAND OF TWO HALVES

The funeral procession begins at the train station. The black-clad mourners huddle like penguins in the five-degree cold and shuffle their way forward along the tramlines. Ahead of the march, the press photographers creep backwards, snapping furiously and trying not to trip over their own feet. The police escort snails dutifully alongside them, the blue lights bringing a rare flash of colour to the grey sky. The coffin, white with a thin black cross, is held up like a standard at the head of the parade. It tilts back at a forty-five-degree angle, beckoning towards the masses behind. Around two thousand mourners have turned out, and they keep a respectful quiet as they trudge around the ring road swigging idly from their beers. Below the casket, the front row holds up a huge black banner with white letters.

In Leipzig stirbt der Fußball. 'Football is dying in Leipzig.'

The mourners are football fans, and they are heading towards the Red Bull Arena, a state-of-the-art modern ground built into the shell of Leipzig's enormous old Zentralstadion. One of Germany's most famous football stadiums, it was built for the 2006 World Cup and has since played host to countless Champions League games, national team fixtures and title deciders. Even on this grey afternoon in January 2020, it doesn't feel like a place where the game is dying. Yet it is also home to RasenBallsport Leipzig. And for the visiting Union Berlin fans, that is reason enough to scream blue murder.

RB Leipzig are one of the most successful teams in Germany. Founded by the drinks company Red Bull in 2009, they have since established themselves alongside Bayern Munich, Borussia Dortmund and Bayer Leverkusen as one of the top four teams in the country. But they are also deeply controversial. As a club whose identity and very existence is dependent on a corporate brand, many see RB as incompatible with the ideas of tradition, identity and community that so many German football fans consider sacred. Their advocates argue that they are a breath of fresh air, who have brought excitement and success back to a once-proud football city. Their critics say they are everything that is wrong with the modern game, which is why the Union Berlin fans have come to symbolically lay football to rest at the Red Bull Arena. As far as they are concerned, Red Bull aren't breathing life back into Leipzig's football. They are zombifying it.

So how did this happen? Are RB really killing football, and if so, then why here of all places? Leipzig, after all, is part of German football's DNA. It was here, in a restaurant just outside the city centre, that the German Football Association (DFB) was founded in 1900, and it was a Leipzig club that became the first ever champions of Germany three years later. This is the birthplace of the German game, the city where the story of the national sport began in earnest. So why have so many people turned out on this cold afternoon to give the game its last rites? How did Leipzig go from being the cradle of German football to being its grave?

For that, you have to understand the city itself. Leipzig lies in the state of Saxony, in the east of Germany near the Czech border. It is one of the most important cities in German history, a centuries-old trade centre which is home to one of the oldest universities in the world and some of the country's most famous sons. It is where Bach composed the *St. John Passion* and Goethe was inspired to write *Faust*. It is also a city that has repeatedly shaped the course of German history, where Prussia and its allies defeated Napoleon, and where tens of thousands of East Germans protested for political change in the autumn of 1989.

Those demonstrations, which took place on the same streets as the funeral march against RB, marked the beginning of Germany as we know it today. They accelerated the fall of the Berlin Wall, which in turn led to the reunification of East and West Germany in 1990. After forty-five years of Cold War division and a century marked by war, genocide and revolution, that moment was the start of a new era for the country. We may think of it as a constant on the European map, but in its current form, with its current borders, Germany is little more than three decades old. And after many failed attempts in the previous two centuries, it is only in the last thirty years that it has thrived as a unified, peaceful democracy.

Yet the decades of division have left their mark. Leipzig may be a major city in German history, but between 1945 and 1990, it belonged to a different Germany entirely. For nearly half a century, it was part of a communist East which developed differently to the capitalist, democratic West. Even now, these two sides of the country still tick differently. People vote differently between East and West, they have different economic prospects and very different family histories. Thirty years on from reunification, Germany is still a land of two halves.

'Football is dying in Leipzig': Union Berlin fans protest against Red Bull in Leipzig in 2020. © Matthias Koch

The difficulties of integrating East and West Germany have also played out in football. Many of the big eastern clubs have struggled since reunification. In Leipzig, 1. FC Lokomotive were once regulars in European competition and a giant of the German game. But they, along with their old cross-town rivals BSG Chemie Leipzig, are now wallowing in the fourth division. For them, as for so many other East German clubs, the years since reunification have been marked by dramatic decline and an uphill struggle to restore past glory.

It wasn't until Red Bull came along that the narrative began to change. When they reached the Bundesliga in 2016, RB Leipzig were the first eastern club in the top flight for seven years. When they won the DFB-Pokal (German Cup) in 2022 and 2023, they were the first eastern club ever to do so. Yet their success always comes with an asterisk. There will always be those who say they are not really an East German club, not really a Leipzig club, not even a proper football club at all.

On one level, this is a squabble over the commercialisation of the beautiful game. And for many, that alone is a matter of footballing life and death. But the fierce debate over RB also gets to the heart of deeper questions about Leipzig and the former East. Thirty years on from the fall of the Berlin Wall, is reunification still a work in progress? What does it mean to be East German in the twenty-first century? And in a country with so many different pasts, how do you shape a common future?

André Göhre is peering through a trap door below the seats of the old wooden grandstand at the Bruno-Plache-Stadion. When they cleared this space out a few years before, he explains, they found cigarette papers, coins and even wallets which had slipped through the floorboards a century earlier. The stand was built in 1923, and it was initially supposed to be a placeholder for a much larger structure. But then hyperinflation hit, and the plans were shelved. The original wooden stand has remained intact ever since and is now a listed building. 'With the exception of the Eiffel Tower, it is the oldest temporary structure in Europe,' says Göhre. He is beaming with pride.

Göhre is the club historian at Lok Leipzig, the fourth-division club who play their home games at the 'Bruno'. He is a short, sturdy man with a big smile and a thick Saxon accent, and he knows the history of football in Leipzig better than almost anyone. Sentences roll out of him in a barrage of dates, names and anecdotes, all at such a pace that he often has to pause to catch his breath. 'It's my job to look after the tradition, to pass it all on to the younger generations and remind people of the history we have here,' he says.

The past matters in German football. For many German fans, the greatest source of pride is not their club's success or their style of play, but their status as a *Traditionsverein*, or a 'traditional club'. It is a term that is used constantly in Germany, and it covers all manner of different teams, from Bayern Munich and Borussia Dortmund in the Bundesliga down to Alemannia Aachen and Kickers Offenbach in the lower leagues. Some Traditionsvereine, like Kaiserslautern or Rot-Weiss Essen, are fallen giants who have not played at the top level for years or even decades. Others, like Arminia Bielefeld or St. Pauli, have never won a national title but can still boast a long history and widespread support in the local area. What unites them all is a sense of continuity and tradition handed down from generation to generation within families, friendship groups and local communities.

Lok Leipzig are arguably the mother of all traditional clubs. They can trace their history back to the 1890s when, under the name of VfB Leipzig, they were among the most important pioneers of organised football in Germany. For much of the twentieth century, the club remained the grandest and most successful club in Leipzig, although you wouldn't know it to look at them now. As he shows me around the crumbling uncovered terraces and the rickety wooden grandstand, Göhre huddles into his jacket to protect himself from the cold April wind. It is a long time since Lok have risen higher than the fourth tier, and their glory days are now a fading memory for most Leipzigers. Göhre is on a mission to preserve that memory. 'People forget that without this city and without this club, there wouldn't be a German football association,' he says defiantly.

Until the dawn of the twentieth century, German football had been a jumbled affair, run by competing regional associations of various sizes without any national oversight. In January 1900, VfB Leipzig's founder and chairman Johannes Kirmse invited representatives from across the country to a meeting at the Zum Mariengarten restaurant, just a few blocks east of where Leipzig's grand main station would be constructed a decade later. Their aim was 'to investigate the possibility of uniting all clubs and associations under one banner', and after hours of fierce debate, the threat of a delayed lunch finally spurred them to a decision. The Deutscher Fußball-Bund (DFB) was born, and three years later, VfB won the association's first ever national championship.

Those events essentially marked the birth of football as Germany's national sport. More than a century on, the DFB is still the national governing body and VfB Leipzig's name is still the first one engraved on the Bundesliga's round, silver trophy. Yet Lok's role in the creation of German football is not widely known outside of Germany, or even outside of Leipzig. Like many East German clubs, their story has been disjointed and obscured by the history of Germany itself.

Lok's Bruno-Plache-Stadion lies in Probstheida, a leafy, residential district in the south-east of Leipzig. In 1813, this was where Prussia and its allies won a decisive victory against Napoleon, beating the French army back towards the west and setting Germany on the road to unification. Until that point, Germany had been more of a cultural and geographical expression than a country. For centuries, the German-speaking lands had existed as part of the Holy Roman Empire, a loose collection of independent kingdoms and duchies with different rulers, currencies and religious leanings. It was only after the Napoleonic Wars that calls for a unified German nation began to emerge across the political spectrum. After a failed liberal and democratic revolution in 1848, the country was ultimately unified under the conservative military might of Prussia in 1871.

This was the start of Germany as a modern nation state, and many essential aspects of modern Germany – from the automobile to the Social Democratic Party – have their roots in the German Empire of 1871–1918. Yet in many ways, this was still a very different country. When the DFB's founders met in Leipzig in 1900, the delegates included representatives from Strasbourg, which is now in France, and took decisions that would affect cities like Breslau and Danzig, which are now Wrocław and Gdansk in Poland. Had VfB Leipzig lost the 1903 final, then the first German champions would have been DFC Prague, a club from a city which was then part of Austro-Hungarian Bohemia and is now the capital of the Czech Republic. At that point, the idea of Germany was still far broader and far more nebulous than the country we know today.

It was also significantly more militaristic. The architect of German unification, Otto von Bismarck, had once declared that history was made "not by speeches and majorities, but by blood and iron", an idea which continued to define the country long into the twentieth century. In 1913, with Kaiser Wilhelm II on the throne and Germany shaping up for another European conflict, a huge memorial was erected in Probstheida to commemorate one hundred years since Napoleon's defeat. The Völkerschlachtsdenkmal (Monument to the Battle of the Nations) still looms over the Bruno-Plache-Stadion today. At ninety-one metres high, it is Europe's tallest monument, a shamelessly bombastic eyesore which portrays a German nation forged at war with France. At the time, that was entirely typical. Nowadays, the monument's jingoism sits a little uncomfortably with modern German sensibilities. For in the years between 1914 and 1945, the country's borders, its society and its very sense of self were to change irrevocably.

Following defeat in the First World War, the Kaiser abdicated and the country was reborn as the Weimar Republic, the first fully democratic German state. Having begun in military defeat and bloody revolution, the Republic's short life was then marked by crippling war reparations, economic crises and political instability. These, in turn, fuelled the rise of the Nazi Party, which ultimately seized power in 1933. For the next twelve years, Germany descended into the darkest period of its history, as Nazi fascism unleashed another world war, committed a monstrous genocide against Europe's Jewish population, and sought to brutally conquer vast swathes of the European continent.

With the Nazis' defeat in 1945, the Allied powers split Germany into four zones of occupation. Leipzig, along with the rest of Saxony and several other eastern regions, fell in the Soviet zone, while the south and west of the country was split between the French, the British and the Americans. After Cold War tensions flared up in 1949, the four blocs became two separate states: the capitalist, democratic Federal Republic of Germany (FRG) in the West, and the communist German Democratic Republic (GDR) in the East. It was at this juncture that VfB Leipzig descended into obscurity and Leipzig's role in the founding of German football was forgotten.

In the West, football returned to the pre-war status quo. The DFB was re-founded in Stuttgart in 1950, and the clubs were also allowed to re-establish under their old names. In the East, it was different. The GDR was not as murderous and tyrannical a regime as the Nazis, but it was still a de facto one-party dictatorship, with a similarly obsessive ideological zeal. The ruling Socialist Unity Party (SED) aimed to build an entirely new society, and that meant throwing out everything that had gone before. In football, a new national association was created, and most of the old football clubs like VfB Leipzig were dissolved or subsumed into newly founded *Sportgemeinschaften* (multi-sport associations). Their former identities, as well as the pre-war history of German football, were deliberately sidelined.

'In the GDR, everything that came before was seen as bad. VfB were traditionally seen as the bourgeois club in Leipzig, and everything bourgeois was demonised. So their historic successes were ignored,' says Göhre. The new East German clubs took their identities not from the past, but from the state-run enterprises with which they were affiliated. Chemie Leipzig were attached to a local producer of paint chemicals. Hansa Rostock, up on the Baltic Sea coast, were the club of the state fisheries. Dynamo Dresden and their Berlin sister club BFC Dynamo were backed by the police department and its notorious state security agency, the Stasi. Like many East

German clubs, the former VfB Leipzig went through several name changes in the first twenty years after the war, as the authorities constantly tinkered with the structures of elite sport. In 1966, they finally became 1. FC Lokomotive Leipzig: the club of the railways.

Lok were one of several clubs who were supposed to help transform the GDR into a footballing power. With East German football lagging behind its western rivals in the 1960s, the authorities moved to reform the club system, channelling resources into ten carefully selected teams in the major cities. But unlike athletics and other Olympic sports, where the regime was able to manufacture success through state-run doping programmes, football proved more difficult to control. In their thirty-eight years as a FIFA member, the East German national team qualified for only one World Cup in 1974, at which they were knocked out in the group stage despite a famous 1–0 win over eventual winners West Germany. In the same year, Magdeburg became the first and only East German club to win a European trophy when they beat AC Milan in the European Cup Winners' Cup final. Beyond that one year of success, East Germany remained a minnow on the international stage.

Yet in domestic football at least, the state's attempts to shape football for its own ends did bear some fruit. As the Stasi became ever more powerful and ramped up its surveillance of East German citizens in the 1970s and 1980s, its favoured football club, BFC Dynamo, also established a firm stranglehold on the GDR Oberliga with ten successive titles from 1979 to 1988. Lok were never that dominant, but they too benefited from a system that pushed the city's best players and facilities into their system. They won their first East German Cup (FDGB-Pokal) in 1976 and soon became one of the few East German teams to enjoy success on the European stage. Göhre's first game, as a six-year-old boy, was in a Cup Winners' Cup match against Tottenham Hotspur in 1974. 'I embarrassed my dad because I was so excited I even celebrated the Spurs goals,' he giggles.

By the late 1980s, Lok were at the height of their power, reaching the Cup Winners' Cup final in 1987 and claiming a fourth FDGB-Pokal win a year later. But by then, the winds of change were beginning to blow through Germany once again. The GDR's economy was in dire straits and its citizens were growing restless. As Mikhail Gorbachev's *Glasnost* reforms began to liberalise the Soviet Union, a burgeoning civil rights movement was pushing for similar change in East Germany. In Leipzig, peace activists started to assemble for Monday prayers at the St. Nicholas Church, and in 1989, those prayer sessions morphed into a 'peaceful revolution', with regular street demonstrations demanding freedom of movement, democratic reform and an end to Stasi tyranny. On 9 October, 70,000 protesters took to the streets of Leipzig chanting: 'We are the people!'

A month later, the GDR opened the border to West Germany, and the Berlin Wall came tumbling down. Amid the wild celebrations and the collapse of the SED's political authority, historical events took on an unstoppable momentum. Within a year, the GDR had collapsed entirely, and the eastern states were officially subsumed into the Federal Republic. German reunification, long dismissed as a political pipe dream, was complete. Now anything seemed possible. As they and other East German clubs rejoined the DFB, Lok briefly rebranded themselves as VfB Leipzig. For half a century under communism, the club's origins as the founders of German football had been ignored, and now they wanted to get back in touch with their roots. As former West German Chancellor Willy Brandt put it in November 1989: 'That which belongs together is growing together again.'

In reality, it wasn't that simple. The division had created two different countries, and it would take more than a few months or years for them to truly grow together. Institutions like the DFB were now firmly rooted in the west and as Göhre points out, 'they had lost their connection to Leipzig'. Even thirty years later, there is little to commemorate the city's role in the birth of German football. The Mariengarten restaurant is long gone, and the building that replaced it bears only a small plaque, which the DFB unveiled in 2000 to mark its own centenary. In the national football museum – which is 400 kilometres away in Dortmund – the founding meeting in Leipzig gets only a passing mention. 'To my mind, that museum should be here, not Dortmund. The DFB wouldn't exist without Leipzig and VfB, but that often gets forgotten in the story they tell about themselves,' grumbles Göhre.

This is a familiar gripe in East German football. For all the huge changes that the West also went through in the twentieth century, there was at least some sense of continuity. The DFB, its national teams and the Bundesliga can all trace their history in a straight line which begins in the early 1900s and goes through the former West Germany into the modern era. The clubs and cities of the East were part of that narrative before and after the Cold War, but between 1945 and 1990 they were cut out of it entirely. While they may be intensely proud of their own history, they also exist in a slightly different timeline to the rest of the German game.

That leaves clubs like Lok with something of a dual identity. At the Bruno-Plache-Stadion, the historic logos of Lok and VfB are often displayed side by side, and the club's official name is now 1. FC Lokomotive VfB Leipzig. 'We are Lok, the three-time East German Cup winners. But we are also VfB, the first ever German champions. We have to honour both sides,' says Göhre. 'That's my job. To pass it on to the younger generations and remind people why Leipzig is known as the secret football capital of Germany.'

The task is all the more important, he argues, given what has happened in Leipzig football since Red Bull's arrival in 2009. Nouveau-riche RB Leipzig are the very opposite of a Traditionsverein, and Göhre wrinkles his nose when he talks about them. Along with other 'non-traditional' clubs like Hoffenheim, Wolfsburg and Bayer Leverkusen, RB's success has been built on corporate investment rather than historical clout. For critics like Göhre, that means they lack something essential. 'The only reason that club exists is to promote their jelly-baby juice, and that has nothing to do with my understanding of what football should be,' says Göhre. 'If all you care about is the money, then you lose something.'

Yet like it or not, the Red Bull model works. For all their history, Lok are no longer top dogs in their city. Instead, it is RB who are flying the flag for Leipzig at the highest level. So how did we get here? Why did RB arrive in the first place, and why are Lok not the ones now playing in the Champions League and challenging for the Bundesliga title? The answer lies in what happened after 1990. And not just in Probstheida, but also on the other side of town.

In the heart of Leipzig's old town, there is a pub called the Auerbachs Keller. A huge wood-panelled beer hall which sits in the cellar of a baroque shopping passage, it has been serving beer and pork on the same spot for 500 years. It was here, as a reluctant law student in the 1760s, that Goethe was supposedly inspired to write *Faust*, his version of a famous old German legend about a scholar who strikes a deal with the devil. The Auerbachs Keller is where the demon Mephisto demonstrates his power to Dr. Faust, terrorising and enchanting the student drinkers in an orgy of song, fire and wine-spouting tables. Faust is convinced and sells his soul in return for endless knowledge and worldly fulfilment.

At the modern Auerbachs Keller, they are still proud of their link to Goethe. In the cellar itself, there is a Goethe room, occasional live performances, and a life-size model of Faust and Mephisto riding out of the pub on a beer barrel. The pre-dinner cocktail bar upstairs is called Mephisto and has a picture of the devil painted on the ceiling. At irregular intervals, the barman presses a button which unleashes a crack of thunder and an evil, cackling laugh from the speakers. It is a gimmick so gloriously naff that it makes even the staff cringe. But it brings in the punters.

And that, too, is what RB Leipzig do. The traditionalists may hate them, but RB still get bums on seats. With Red Bull's money behind them, they have done what Lok and the other Leipzig clubs failed to do and brought success back to the birthplace of German football. Since they arrived in Leipzig in the mid-to-late 2000s, the city has rapidly re-established itself as one of the most important football centres in the country. Before they arrived, it was in a state of permacrisis.

Jens Fuge sighs when he thinks back to that time. 'I do think Red Bull picked their moment very well,' he says. 'The traditional clubs in Leipzig were nowhere, and they had proved they couldn't get it together.' A white-haired motorbike enthusiast in his early sixties, Fuge is a lifelong fan of Chemie Leipzig, Lok's traditional cross-city rivals. Like Lok, Chemie boast a proud history and a once huge fanbase, and in another universe, they might have become what RB are now. Instead, their experience of the post-reunification era has been, much like that of many other former East German clubs, a rollercoaster ride of name changes, insolvencies and endless infighting, in which early optimism soon descended into total failure. As a journalist, club historian and occasional board member, Fuge saw his club's dramatic decline from almost every possible angle.

He has been following Chemie since the 1970s, when they and Lok were on opposing sides of a lopsided GDR rivalry. Lok, in well-to-do south-eastern Probstheida, were the local superpower. Chemie, from working-class Leutzsch in the north-west, played the eternal second fiddle. While Lok attracted all the best players in the city, Chemie were left to pick up the scraps, and when they won the title in 1964, people joked that they had done so with 'the rest of Leipzig'. For their fans, the phrase was a badge of pride, a sign that they were the good guys in an unjust system. At least in the folklore of football, that idea stuck: Lok were the state team. Chemie were the rebels.

From a western perspective, the history of East Germany is often cast in these terms: the state and the resistance, the good guys and the bad guys. Fuge warns against overstating the narrative. 'There was a whiff of rebellion to football fandom back then, but words like "resistance" are too strong. Resistance was what people did to fight the Nazis. It wasn't the same in the GDR,' he says. His own biography is a good example of how many East

German stories are far more nuanced and contradictory. As a teenager, he was blackmailed into becoming a Stasi informant. As a young man, he became involved in the reform movements and was eventually granted permission to leave for the West. This was a country where the line between state and citizen, victim and perpetrator, was not always clear cut. It was also, Fuge notes, a place where many people lived happy lives. 'My wife has a very different view of the GDR to me, for example, because she never had any trouble with the authorities.'

But it is not just people's experience of the GDR itself that defines their opinion of it. It is also their experience of what came after it. For some, the fall of the Wall and German reunification brought deliverance from state terror under an oppressive regime. For others, it brought a sudden onslaught of uncertainty, instability and economic turmoil. Chemie are a good example of both.

When the GDR ceased to exist in 1990, many East German clubs were hopeful of a bright new future ahead. The sense of optimism and excitement led many to change their names, with Lok rebranding as VfB, Wismut Aue becoming Erzgebirge Aue and BFC Dynamo switching to FC Berlin. 'People were getting divorced, losing their jobs, starting new lives. Everything that was once certain was being destroyed, and anything that reminded people of the GDR was suddenly undesirable,' says Fuge. Chemie, whose name evoked the horrendous environmental damage and water pollution inflicted by the GDR's coal and uranium industries, were no different. In August 1990, they rebranded as FC Sachsen Leipzig, a name which had echoes of Bayern Munich in its combination of state and city. 'That was the spirit. There was this hope that without the

GDR system, which had always held Chemie back, the chains would be off and we could really do something big,' says Fuge.

In reality, reunification proved to be a much bumpier ride. The same industries that had poisoned Leipzig's air and water supply were now being wound up, leaving many people out of work. Unemployment, which had officially not existed under socialism, now soared as the GDR's creaking industries were wound down and privatised. By the end of the 1990s, almost one in five people were out of work in the former East.[1] Meanwhile, the new FC Sachsen were one of many eastern teams who failed to secure a place in the new unified Bundesliga, and crowd numbers soon began to dwindle. People had other things on their minds than football, and the game was also plagued by the hooliganism and extremism which had developed among some East German fan scenes in the late 1980s. As the two German police forces were hastily merged in 1990, violence and lawlessness reigned in many stadiums. In November 1990, an FC Berlin fan named Mike Polley was shot dead by police at a game against FC Sachsen.

The years that followed would bring many more false dawns. In the 1990s and 2000s, various club presidents hailed ill-fated strategies to make FC Sachsen 'a speedboat to the second division' and 'a new football Mecca for the East'. Instead, the club repeatedly squandered the investment and good faith that was continuously pumped into them. Fuge's memoirs include tales of player transfers being completed in car parks with carrier bags full of cash and shady marketing subsidiaries paying absurdly inflated salaries to club employees. By the end, he says, FC Sachsen were a laughing stock. 'The people in charge had squandered all the trust that anyone had in them and made every mistake it is possible to make in professional football,' he says bitterly.

FC Sachsen's failure was also a problem for the city. In the early 2000s, the huge GDR-era Zentralstadion had been renovated at great expense in order to host the 2006 World Cup. To avoid being lumped with a white elephant after the tournament, Leipzig needed a successful club to occupy the new stadium. Lok, who had briefly reached the Bundesliga as VfB in the early 1990s, had since gone bust and re-founded themselves in the lower leagues. FC Sachsen who moved into the stadium in 2003, were in similarly dire straits and struggled to fill the 40,000-capacity arena. By the time RB were founded in 2009, the city was desperate for anyone who could take the stadium off their hands. As Leipzig fan activist Matthias Gärtner remarked to *Der Spiegel* that year: 'Red Bull have come to a football city in a state of utter desolation. At this point, the devil himself could come knocking and if he had a few million euros, people would welcome him with open arms.'

Having already founded clubs in Austria, the USA and Brazil, Red Bull had long been looking to break into the German market, and Leipzig was tailor-made for their purposes. It had football history, a ready-made stadium, and an obvious vacuum to be filled. Initially, in 2006, the drinks company made a bid to buy out FC Sachsen, but they were met with fierce resistance from the club's fans, who stubbornly rejected any proposal to change the club's identity once again. The Faustian pact fell through and Sachsen went bust a few years later, leaving a splinter club to re-found under the old name of Chemie. Red Bull, meanwhile, took a different tack entirely. In 2009, they bought the league licence from suburban minnows SSV Markranstädt and rebranded the team as RasenBallsport Leipzig.

A deal with the devil: in a statue outside the Auerbachs Keller in Leipzig, Mephistopheles demonstrates his power to Faust. © Kit Holden

The name was a fudge, designed to maintain the initials 'RB' without breaking the DFB's sponsorship rules, which prohibit the use of commercial sponsors in a club's official name or emblem. In every other regard, the new club was exactly like all the others in Red Bull's global football network. They wore the same white shirts with red shorts, with the same company logo blazoned across it. Their mascot was a red bull, the official nickname was 'the Red Bulls', and the Zentralstadion was rebranded as the Red Bull Arena. 'They took football, which is such an important emotional thing for so many people, and turned it into a marketing tool,' says Fuge. Like many fans, he is appalled by this notion of a purely corporate football club. 'For me, a football club is more than just a team. It's everything around it: the employees, the fans and the members,' he says.

Alongside tradition, membership is one of German football's sacred cows. German fan culture is built around the idea that fans can become members of their club, allowing them to elect directors, challenge the leadership, and even run for office themselves. As of 2023, more than two million Germans were members of a professional football club, with Bayern Munich alone having 300,000. The 50+1 rule, which was introduced as football became ever more commercial in the late 1990s, was designed to protect member influence over their clubs. It stipulates that, regardless of a club's ownership structure, members must retain majority voting rights, effectively meaning clubs are directly accountable to their fans. On paper, RB Leipzig abide by the rule. Yet in practice, they have only twenty voting members as of 2023. Though RB fans can in principle apply for membership, the fees are so high and the process so obfuscatory that none do. It is a system that observes the letter of the 50+1 rule while simultaneously trampling all over the spirit of it.

For the tens of thousands of Leipzigers who go to watch RB every week, that is a price worth paying. RB delivered on their promise of success, reaching the top flight within seven years and getting to the Champions League semi-finals in 2020. After years without a top-flight team, Fuge says it is understandable that many people have given up on Lok and Chemie and started flocking to the new kids on the block. 'RB fans aren't aliens,' he says with a wink. 'A lot of people were really disappointed with the old clubs, and they were just happy to see some high-level football in Leipzig again. Money tends to win out in our capitalist society, and we're not going to change that. From a marketing perspective, there is a lot to admire about Red Bull, and there is no doubt that RB are good for the city in economic terms.'

Yet he insists that member-owned clubs like Chemie and Lok offer something more valuable: a sense of social cohesion. 'As a football fan, you have a choice. Do I just want to see successful football, or do I want to actually have a say in how things are done?' Chemie may now be in the fourth tier, he says, but it is also a community club that is owned by and run by its supporters in the truest sense. 'We do everything ourselves. That's something we can be proud of. It makes people identify with the club, and that puts us miles ahead of RB fans.'

In the end, it comes down to perspective. Is football merely entertainment, or is it part of the very fabric of society, of a region's identity? That is a particularly loaded question in eastern Germany, where regional identity is so intimately tied up with the history of the GDR. East Germany may have ceased to exist as a state in 1990, but that was not the end of East German history. Thirty years on from reunification, many people in the former GDR still identify very strongly as East German – even those who were born long after the Wall came down.

It is quiet on derby day. Though it has boomed in recent decades, Leipzig is still only now getting close to its pre-war high of around 700,000 residents. Away from the historic centre, it can still feel eerily empty. Yet on this particular Sunday in Leutzsch, tension is brewing beneath the quiet. Police drones and a helicopter hover above the rooftops. Squads of riot police, some on horseback, line the pavements and the street corners. It is a lot of officers for a fourth-tier regional league game with only 5000 spectators. But this isn't just any old game. Today, Lok are playing Chemie. And the city is on edge.

Just like Lok's Bruno-Plache-Stadion, Chemie's Alfred-Kunze-Sportpark has seen better days. The paths that guide the fans through the woods are muddy, and full of potholes. Today's game is sold out, but the main grandstand looks half full. Many of the seats are in such bad condition that nobody can sit on them, which means most simply mill around in the walkways. The home end rises like an abandoned Mayan temple above the goal, a 1980s digital scoreboard perched on top of its crumbling concrete steps. It is a long way from the slick, space-age feel of the Red Bull Arena up the road. And it has been a long time since Lok and Chemie were the pride of this city.

Yet some things don't change, and these two still hate each other. Ahead of kick-off, banners are raised at both ends of the stadium. The visiting Lok fans call on each other to 'fight the enemy' and wish death and destitution on their city rivals. The Chemie fans cheerfully call their guests 'sons of whores'. Violent clashes are not uncommon, which is why the police are out in force. There is a political undercurrent as well: Lok's fans have a reputation for right-wing extremism, while Chemie's leading ultra groups are firmly on the left. Yet ultimately, this is a historic grudge, with roots in the GDR. The Lok fans hold up a banner with '1966', the year they were founded by the East German state. The Chemie fans sing about their GDR Oberliga title win in 1964, the golden hour of the famous 'Rest of Leipzig'.

'The history of the GDR still plays a huge role in East German identity. Especially as football fans, we hark back to it constantly,' says Alexander Mennicke. Mennicke is a football writer and researcher who has written extensively on fan culture in the former eastern bloc. He is also a member of one of Chemie's main ultra groups, meaning that on derby day, he is part of the pulsating mass of green-and-white flags in the home end.

'Ultra' is an often misunderstood term in the English-speaking world. One thing it is not is a synonym for 'hooligan', even if the two subcultures occasionally overlap. Hooliganism is, by definition, the pursuit of organised violence. Ultra culture, which originated in Italy and spread across Europe in the 1990s, is about collective and unconditional support for a team. Ultras are the ones who create the atmosphere, leading the chants and designing the dramatic 'tifo' artworks which are unfurled ahead of big games. They also serve as the ideological arm of a club's fanbase, staging protests and demonstrations on supporter rights and political issues, and engaging in social and community projects. In Germany, there are ultra groups from across the political spectrum, from the far right to the hard left. Whatever their persuasion, ultras tend to see themselves not just as supporters, but as guardians of the tradition and the identity of their club. And as Mennicke says, at a club like Chemie, that identity has a lot to do with the GDR.

Mennicke was born in 1986 and was only three years old when the Berlin Wall came down. Many of his fellow ultras are even younger and know the communist era only from their parents' recollections. Yet for many, the East is still the East. Mennicke talks about 'phantom borders' – the idea that historical countries or regions continue to exist on a cultural level long after they officially disappear. In East German football, the decline of the grand old clubs means that the modern north-eastern regional league often looks eerily like the old GDR top flight. While the big East German clubs have remained stuck in the lower division, the Bundesliga and 2. Bundesliga are still made up mostly of western clubs. 'You only need to look at the top two divisions and where the clubs come from to see there is still a border of sorts in football,' says Mennicke.

On the terraces, many fans in the former East have actively embraced that border. Fans of Dynamo Dresden often chant 'East, East, East Germany!' when they travel to away games in the West, while they and other ultra groups frequently hang a GDR flag on the fence in front of their block. As Mennicke points out, much of this is just provocation for provocation's sake. But as someone who has interviewed football fans across the region, he also sees a deeper common thread. 'Some people identify very clearly as East Germans, others would maybe say they are East Berliners. The thing that unites everyone, even those born after reunification, is the sense that they are in some way from "the East". For me, being East German is something you are born with, you can't do anything about it.'

The collapse of communism may have been a cause for celebration for most East Germans, but many still have fond memories of their childhood and teenage years in the GDR. Often, this sort of thing is dismissed as *Ostalgie* or 'East nostalgia': a rose-tinted view of the East's dark history. Yet feeling East German is not the same as wanting communism back, and even for those who suffered under the regime, the GDR was still the country they called home. Likewise, those born into reunified Germany have also had a different life experience to their counterparts in the West.

For a start, they are less well off. The GDR's state industries were privatised en masse after reunification, with many bought up and rationalised by western investors. The legacy of that process is hotly disputed, but what is certain is that it left a lot of people out of a job. Unemployment remained at about twenty per cent in the East until the mid-2000s and is still far higher than in most western regions. Coupled with the public money that flooded into the eastern states in the 2000s, that economic imbalance has provided fertile ground for terrace humour. Union Berlin's official club anthem includes a tongue-in-cheek line about 'never being bought by the West'. In the early 2000s, Chemie fans used to chant 'We come from the East and we live at your expense!' when they played against western opposition.

More sinisterly, football has also reflected the East's tendency towards political extremes. Both the hard-left Linke party and the far-right Alternative für Deutschland (AfD) have traditionally polled highly in the East, while populist protest movements against immigration and Covid regulations often mobilise particularly high numbers in eastern cities. The hooliganism which had thrived on East German terraces in the late 1980s also fed in to the shocking outbreaks of racist violence which swept the East after reunification. In Rostock in the summer of 1992, neo-Nazis launched a violent arson attack on an asylum centre and a block housing Vietnamese migrant workers. One picture from the riots, showing a man in a Germany football shirt and soiled trousers raising his arm in a Nazi salute, would burn itself into the national consciousness for years to come. Even now, far-right tendencies are not uncommon in East German fan culture. In 2019, Chemnitz fans publicly mourned a local neo-Nazi at a regional league game, while BFC Dynamo and Energie Cottbus have also been fined over racist incidents involving supporters in recent years.

These problems are not unique to the East. Yet they are a fundamental part of the region's troubled recent history, which is partly why East German identity remains such a thorny issue. Mennicke argues that amid the unemployment and economic hardship after reunification, many eastern fan groups naturally developed a more violent, more aggressive self-image. The narrative of an East toughened by the hardship of dictatorship and economic inferiority is an enticing one for many people. 'In modern Germany, there aren't any political parties or major institutions that are originally or exclusively East German, but the football clubs are,' he says. Most eastern clubs play up to this on some level. Even RB Leipzig stylise themselves as 'The Pride of the East'.

That is a sore point, of course. Geographically, Leipzig is in the former East. But unlike the other clubs, RB have no roots in the GDR. 'In reality, they are a club created by an Austrian brand and planted here artificially,' says Mennicke. 'In that sense, you could argue they are exactly the thing that people have been moaning about in the East for years: Westerners coming over with their money and doing what they like, almost like a form of colonialism.' He hastens to add that he doesn't see it in those terms. Yet he does see RB as an 'external, elite project'.

In the end, it comes back to how you tell history. 'When we talk about tradition in football, we are ultimately talking about collective memory, shared values and experiences,' says Mennicke.

RB, by definition, cannot tap in to that collective memory in the same way a traditional club like Chemie, Lok or Dynamo Dresden can. 'RB have East German fans. But for me, they are not an East German club,' he says. Yet at the same time, he also warns against insisting on tradition for tradition's sake. 'If I say "tradition", do I also mean the fact that many of these old clubs were part of the GDR system, founded by the regime and run by party members and Stasi officials? Do I also mean all the racist, right-wing songs which were sung in East German stadiums in the 1980s, 1990s and even the 2000s? Those aren't traditions I particularly want to keep alive. Tradition is important, but you have to apply it to the here and now,' he says.

That, when it comes down to it, is the ongoing challenge of German reunification. In many ways, it doesn't necessarily help to portray the East as a victim of history or an eternal problem child. At the same time, the modern East does have a different story, one that cannot be ignored or wished away. Given the horrors of German history, it is a miracle that the country emerged as a unified, peaceful democracy in the twenty-first century. The thousands of peaceful protesters who took to the streets in Leipzig in 1989 played their part in that miracle. Yet thirty years on, the legacy of communism and the division still looms large. To some extent, Germany still has two faces.

Ironically, that is particularly true at the Red Bull Arena. From the inside, RB Leipzig's stadium looks like almost any other modern entertainment venue, one which could just as well be in Munich, Cologne, London or Paris. To get inside the stadium, however, you have to pass through the gates of the huge 1950s Zentralstadion, built as a prestige project at the height of communist power. The walkways into the new stadium are suspended above the landscaped slopes of the old one, where 110,000 people once flocked to see East Germany take on Czechoslovakia.

The two stadiums are in exactly the same place. Yet they were also built in two completely different countries. Likewise, the DFB may have been founded in Leipzig, a city in the East. But it is also the football association of the Federal Republic of Germany. And the story of that country begins in the West.

THE RHINELAND

- MÖNCHENGLADBACH
- DÜSSELDORF
- COLOGNE

2

THE RHINELAND
JESTERS AND KINGS

Ingo Reipka has one of the most important jobs in Cologne. Every other Saturday, he goes to the zoo, bundles a ninety-four-kilogram billy goat into the back of a van, and drives to the RheinEnergieStadion in Müngersdorf. Once there, he is escorted through a sea of selfie-hunters into the bowels of the stadium, where the animal is dressed up with a leash and a smart red tabard. Shortly before kick-off, man and goat scamper out onto the pitch through a guard of cheerleaders in front of 50,000 adoring fans, goat noises bleating out from the speakers as they go. 'It's pretty spectacular. I get goosebumps every time,' says Reipka.

German football has its fair share of eccentric mascots. RB Leipzig's red bull 'Bulli' looks like a retired wrestler with a spiralling cocaine habit. Bayern Munich used to have 'Bazi' – a nightmarish, rosy-cheeked Bavarian country bumpkin in lederhosen – until he was mercifully retired in 2004. Schalke's 'Erwin' is best described as an oversized nose with a cap and a mullet, and is, by the club's own admission, 'neither human nor animal'. But only one club – 1. FC Köln – has a live goat on the touchline. His name is Hennes IX and he is something of a local celebrity.

'Hennes is as iconic as the cathedral. You can't imagine Cologne without him,' says Reipka.

Köln have had a goat mascot since 1950, just two years after the club was founded. The first animal was gifted to them by a local circus director during Carnival, and urban legend has it that it promptly cocked a leg on player-coach Hennes Weisweiler, earning itself the name Hennes. When it died in 1966, a new goat was found and duly christened Hennes II. Thus began a long line of Henneses, some of whom have brought the club more luck than others.

Reipka has been Köln's official goat-minder since 2006, when Hennes VII was still around. He is now in charge of Hennes IX, who is bigger and more boisterous than some of his predecessors. 'Sometimes, when we are sitting on the touchline watching the game, he tries to headbutt my chair – I think because it's green and he doesn't like the colour,' says Reipka. 'But the thing he most likes to do is eat. So as long as I have a good supply of pellets and carrots and stuff, it's fine.' The only downside to the job is that he can never stay until the final whistle. 'I have to go at least ten minutes before full time, otherwise I'd never make it out of the car park with all the crowds.'

Hennes, after all, is an icon in these parts. 'When people see him, they flip out,' says Reipka. 'When I was first offered the job, I had to think hard about it because I knew I would be in the public eye.' Even on non-matchdays, it is a demanding job, with Hennes making regular appearances at weddings, birthday parties and other events. The goat has also become an on-screen star, appearing on talk shows and TV crime dramas. At 1. FC Köln, his image is everywhere, from the fan shop to the players' tunnel, where a picture of his hindquarters taunts the away team

Hennes IX, Köln's famous goat mascot, with his minder Ingo Reipka at a women's Bundesliga game in 2023. © 1. FC Köln

as they head out onto the pitch. The club's official HQ is known as the *Geißbockheim*, or 'Billy Goat Home', and their nickname is the 'Billy Goats'. Hennes is even on the club badge, perched with his front legs on top of the two spires of the city's famous cathedral.

The badge is Cologne in a nutshell. On the one hand, it is one of Germany's most important cities, the centre of Catholic power in the country and an ancient centre of trade and culture, home to one of the most famous church buildings in the world. On the other hand, it is a city where a circus goat can become a folk hero. *Kölner* are famous for not taking life too seriously, for their good-natured hospitality and, most importantly, for their Carnival.

They call Carnival the 'fifth season' in Cologne. Officially, it begins at eleven minutes past eleven on 11 November, but the main festivities take place in the week leading up to Lent. Revellers known as *Jecken* or *Narren* take to the streets in their hundreds of thousands in fancy dress for a week-long whirlwind of parties, parades and other events held by the dozens of official Carnival associations. It is an orgy of organised fun, political satire and plain silliness, and one in which the football club gets fully involved. Köln players are expected to take part in the parades and turn up to training in fancy dress, while the club releases a special-edition 'Carnival shirt' every single season. On the pitch, too, they have developed a reputation as the quintessential 'Carnival club'. In recent decades, Köln have lurched from crisis to crisis with comic regularity, being relegated from the Bundesliga no fewer than five times between 2000 and 2018.

Carnival – also known as Fasching or Fastnacht – is not just celebrated in Cologne. There are versions of it in countless German cities, from the Dutch border down to the furthest south-eastern corners of Bavaria. Yet the heartland of Carnival is in the Rhineland, a loosely defined region in the far west of Germany which encompasses cities like Cologne, Düsseldorf, Mönchengladbach and Aachen. Officially, these places are all in the federal state of North Rhine-Westphalia. But if you ask most people around this region how they identify, they will say they are Rhinelanders. And while the Rhineland has no clearly defined borders per se, it is a region which has shaped German history like few others.

The Rhine, which flows from the Swiss Alps up through western Germany to the North Sea, has always had a particular hold on the German imagination. It was once a key frontier of ancient Europe, separating the Roman-controlled west from the Germanic tribes of the east. Centuries later, the stories of plucky German tribesmen beating back the advancing Romans would be gleefully picked up by German nationalists, who were themselves engaged in a decades-long series of border disputes with the French. While France long claimed the Rhine as a natural border, the necessity to maintain territory on both sides of the river became a founding principle of early German nationhood.

Wherever you drew the border, however, the Rhineland was always where Germany met the rest of Western Europe. It was the Romans who built cities like Cologne, Aachen and Trier, and those cities continued to look south and west long after the Empire itself had fallen. In the sixteenth century, when Martin Luther unleashed the Protestant Reformation which divided Germany and Europe on religious lines, the Rhineland remained defiantly Roman Catholic. One of Luther's reforms was to abolish Carnival, and even now, Germany's confessional divide can be traced on those terms. Carnival and Fasching are celebrated almost exclusively in the Catholic south and west. In the Lutheran north and east people tend to screw up their noses and grit their teeth at the mere mention of them.

There are exceptions, of course. Reipka, a northerner who moved to Cologne in the 1980s, has bought wholesale in to the culture of his adopted Rhineland home. 'It's a beautiful region, and I like the mentality here,' he says. 'People are open-hearted, they tell you what they think, and they don't pretend to be something they're not.'

Yet that is only half the story. The Rhineland is more than Carnival, and 1. FC Köln are more than just a quirky club with a cuddly mascot. They are also one of German football's great grandees, a club without which the Bundesliga would never have been founded and Germany may not have developed into the footballing power it later became. In their glory years between the 1950s and 1980s, they and other Rhineland clubs like Fortuna Düsseldorf and Borussia Mönchengladbach shaped the modern German game and produced some of its most influential players and managers. At the same time, the region was also shaping modern Germany. It was here, in the rolling hills of the west, where Germany was reborn politically after the horrors of Nazism, where it finally made lasting peace with France and reimagined itself as a democratic nation. The Rhineland, in short, was the cradle of West Germany and therefore of the modern German state. In politics as in football, it was always a country of both jesters and kings.

When you arrive in Cologne, the first thing you see is the *Dom*. The city's monumental Gothic cathedral looms over the train station like a cliff face, and you have to strain your neck to follow the twin spires as they rise to the heavens. At 156 metres, it is both the tallest cathedral in the world and the tallest church building with two spires. Only the Sagrada Familia, Gaudi's unfinished masterpiece in Barcelona, is designed to be taller, and that has been under construction for nearly 150 years.

Still, these things take time. Cologne's *Dom* was started in 1248 and built piece by piece for several centuries before work was abandoned in the 1500s. It was only in the nineteenth century, when the Romantics took up the cause of Gothic architecture, that construction continued. By the time it was finally completed in 1880, the Catholic Church was embroiled in a bitter political struggle with the new imperial German government, and remained largely absent from the festivities. Nowadays, though, the church is the pride of Catholic Germany and the symbol of the country's fourth-largest city. As people here say: 'Home is where the *Dom* is.'

The fact that it is still standing at all borders on a miracle. Though Cologne is technically a Roman city, the medieval cathedral is still by far and away one of its oldest buildings. Cologne was one of the most heavily bombed cities in Europe in the Second World War, and an estimated seventy per cent of its Roman old town was destroyed during the course of the conflict.[2] From the RAF's '1000 bomber raid' of May 1942 to the relentless bombardment in October 1944, Allied bombs decimated the city and forced many of its inhabitants to spend the last months of the war almost completely underground. Whether by divine intervention, architectural genius or sheer luck, the *Dom* survived the onslaught and was almost the last thing standing in 1945.

'I grew up playing in the bombed-out ruins,' says Wolfgang Niedecken, one of Cologne's most famous musicians. 'I played

The Kölner Dom, or Cologne Cathedral, is the third tallest church building in the world. © Kit Holden

in rubble even before I had any idea what rubble really was. I guess I just thought of it like an adventure playground. It was only when I got a bit older that I started asking: "Why is everything broken around here?"'

In the first months and years after the war, it was often ordinary German women who cleared the wreckage from the city streets. These so-called *Trümmerfrauen* or 'rubble ladies' quickly became icons of Germany's post-war rebuild, but even by the time Niedecken was born in 1951, the scars of the bombing campaigns still ran deep in the city, its topography and its collective psyche. 'The people in my parents' generation lived through terrible things. They had to start again from zero,' he says.

Nonetheless, he remembers his own childhood as 'idyllic'. Niedecken grew up in the south of Cologne, where his parents ran a grocery store. The economic effects of the US Marshall Plan were beginning to kick in when he was born, and his youth was marked by the 'economic miracle' that revitalised West Germany from the 1950s to the 1970s. As the frontman of the rock band BAP, he would become one of the iconic voices of his generation, merging his native Cologne dialect with the sound of English rock'n'roll and American folk rock. Niedecken became known as the 'Bob Dylan of the Südstadt' after the Cologne neighbourhood where he grew up.

Besides the physical and economic rebuilding, post-war West Germany was also attempting to construct a new German state from the rubble of Nazism and war. While the SED and their Soviet backers were establishing the GDR in the East, the French, British and American zones in the West had merged into the Federal Republic of Germany (FRG) in 1949. After the failures of the Frankfurt assembly in the mid-nineteenth century and the Weimar Republic of 1919–33, this was the third attempt to establish liberal democracy on German soil and it was by no means predestined to succeed. In 1949, open questions still loomed large over West Germany: Could the FRG's citizens be transformed from Nazis into democrats? Should it seek to reunify with the East or remain divided? And would it stay neutral or take a side in the brewing Cold War? The answers, to a large extent, would be hashed out in the Rhineland.

One of the first issues that faced the new state was where the seat of government should be. Berlin, divided and isolated far in the East, was out of the question, which meant a suitable replacement would have to be found in the West. Initially, it seemed Frankfurt was the frontrunner, but when it came to the vote in the provisional parliamentary council, it was the city of Bonn, just south of Cologne, that came out on top. The architect of this surprise victory was Bonn MP and former Cologne mayor Konrad Adenauer, the man who would soon be elected Germany's first post-war Chancellor.

Adenauer had been a leading politician for the Catholic Centre Party in pre-war Germany, serving sixteen years as Cologne mayor before the Nazis effectively removed him from power in 1933. A proud Rhinelander, he had always been deeply sceptical of militaristic Prussian hegemony and, in a speech in 1919, had railed against what he called 'the rule of Germany by the spirit of the east'. After the Second World War, having helped found the new centre-right Christian Democratic Union, he set about integrating the new Germany into the wider West. As Chancellor, he quickly and decisively positioned the Federal Republic on the side of the US and its allies and began to build strong economic ties with France and the Low Countries. At the same time, the Marshall Plan was helping to turbo-charge the economy of Western Europe, bolstering Adenauer's pro-Western, anti-communist course. The Chancellor, who was already seventy-three when he took office in 1949, led his party to thumping victories in three more elections, racking up an astonishing fourteen years in power.

It wasn't until the summer of 1954 that the country had its first big cultural moment, and when it came, it came on the football pitch. At the World Cup in Switzerland, West Germany went into the final as rank outsiders against a legendary Hungary team who had thrashed them once already in the group stage. But in Bern, the Germans pulled off a dramatic smash-and-grab 3–2 victory thanks to a late winner from striker Helmut Rahn. The celebrations and the famous radio commentary quickly became part of the cultural folklore of the new West Germany, prompting decades of books, documentaries and screen dramatisations. The historian Joachim Fest would later remark that the Federal Republic had three founding fathers: Adenauer, his successor Ludwig Erhard, and the World Cup winning captain, Fritz Walter.

Niedecken was too young to remember the 'Miracle of Bern', but it still held a powerful sway over his generation of football fans. Hans Schäfer, the Cologne winger whose cross set up Rahn's winning goal, would soon become his childhood hero, kickstarting a lifelong love affair with 1. FC Köln. 'When I was small, my father and my half-brother would listen to football on the radio. They would be completely transfixed by it, and every time Hans Schäfer did anything for Köln or the national team, there would be this huge celebration,' he says. 'I'd listen and then go out on the street to re-enact the goals I'd heard on the radio. And I would always be Hans Schäfer.'

It was no surprise that Köln had a World Cup hero among their ranks. The western regions of Germany were also establishing themselves as a footballing powerbase in the post-war period, and Köln were a club that had been founded with the express intention of winning titles. 'Do you want to join me and become German champions?' was the club founder Franz Kremer's famous sales pitch when he persuaded two local teams, SpVgg Sülz 07 and Kölner BC 01, to join forces in 1948. The merger produced 1. FC Köln, or 'First FC Cologne', the club that would become the undisputed darling of the Carnival city. In truth, they were neither the first nor the only club around: VfL Köln could boast a longer history and Fortuna Köln also spent a few years in the Bundesliga in the 1960s. Yet even Fortuna never really achieved popularity beyond the south of the city, and Cologne always had the feel of a one-club town. Today, 1. FC Köln loom so large that they are known to fans and rivals alike simply as 'FC'.

Franz Kremer's vision of glory, meanwhile, became reality remarkably quickly. Köln were crowned German champions in 1962, a mere decade and a half after they were founded. At the same time, they and their president played a key role in the creation of the Bundesliga, Germany's first professional national league. Until 1963, the German championship had been split into four regional leagues, the winners of which would compete in an end-of-season play-off for the title. This was seen as a disadvantage in comparison with countries like Italy, Spain and England, whose professional nationwide leagues had produced some of the greatest teams of the day. Alongside 1954 World Cup winning coach Sepp Herberger, Kremer lobbied hard for the Bundesliga, which his club promptly won in its inaugural season in 1963/4. As they wowed the new TV audiences with their bright white shirts and silky style of play in the early 1960s, they were soon nicknamed the 'Real Madrid of the Rhineland'.

That success only cemented Niedecken's love for the club, and, as he tells it, it was his obsession with 1. FC Köln that ultimately launched his career as a rockstar. He and a friend founded BAP in the summer of 1976, the morning after West Germany beat Yugoslavia in the semi-final of the European Championships with goals from Köln players Heinz Flohe and Dieter Müller. Had he not been so flustered and hungover after the wild celebrations, he chuckles, he might have been sensible enough not to form the band. As it was, BAP soon made it big, releasing their breakthrough album three years later and going on to record more number one albums in Germany than the Beatles. Perhaps even more impressively, they did so by singing in *Kölsch*, the local dialect spoken in Cologne. 'I was probably lovesick when I started writing songs, and you express your emotions best in your mother tongue,' explains Niedecken. 'Kölsch is still the only language I speak perfectly. Until I was six, we only spoke Kölsch at home, and the first foreign language I learned at school was standard German.'

Cologne is not unique in this regard. Standard German, which was codified partly as a result of Luther's Reformation, is above all a written language, and it has countless spoken variations across the German-speaking world. Some, like Berlinish, are essentially a developed form of slang. Others, like Swiss German, are practically a separate tongue. Kölsch is somewhere in between: vaguely comprehensible to other German-speakers, but also markedly different in sound, rhythm and grammar. Its gravelly fluidity is also more suitable to rock'n'roll, and BAP were not the only band to take advantage of that. Alongside others like Bläck Fööss and Zeltlinger Band, they were part of a wave of 'Kölschrock' bands which emerged in the 1970s and enjoyed success far beyond Cologne and the Rhineland. 'Standard German is an incredibly unmusical language. If you try to express your emotions in it, you end up sounding bureaucratic,' chuckles Niedecken.

Yet standard German has also become more and more powerful in recent decades. As Germans have moved around a lot more in a globalised world, many regional dialects have begun to die out. In Cologne, it is arguably only the holy trinity of *Kölschrock*, *Karneval* and 1. FC Köln that has kept the local language in such rude health. From the terrace chants to the official club hymn 'Mer stonn zo dir, FC Kölle', Kölsch is the lingua franca at the stadium in Müngersdorf. 'We are the only club in Germany whose fans only sing in dialect, and we are pretty proud of that. We had a player once called Matthias Scherz, who moved from St. Pauli to Köln. I remember he said that for an away team player, it was like a kind of voodoo when the whole stadium was singing in a language you didn't understand,' says Niedecken. He himself remembers being moved to tears when the fans spontaneously broke out into the Bläck Fööss song 'In unserem Veedel' after a defeat in the 2000s.

By that point, defeats had become far more common. Until reunification, Köln had maintained their status as one of the major powers of German football, with five top-three finishes in the 1980s and a DFB-Pokal win in 1983. Yet as the millennium loomed, their aura began to wane. In 1990, they sold Germany midfielder Thomas Häßler to Juventus for a record 14 million deutschmarks and sacked highly successful head coach Christoph Daum. That marked the start of a decade of mistakes and mismanagement which would change the club's status forever. Despite the notorious 'Häßler millions', Köln still found themselves in crippling debt a year later and went on to sell several other key players over the course of the 1990s. In 1998, Niedecken remembers sitting on his motorcycle outside a gig and crying his eyes out after the club were relegated from the Bundesliga for the first time in their history. Though they bounced back two years later, the glory years were gone for good.

Their popularity, though, has remained unscathed. Despite several seasons in the second division, Köln have consistently drawn crowds of between forty thousand and fifty thousand throughout the twenty-first century, making them one of Germany's most well-attended clubs. When Köln were relegated in 2018, the fans sang Carnival songs in the away block at Freiburg. In the second division the following year, attendances actually increased. For Niedecken, the loyalty and levity of the Köln fans is typical of the city itself. 'People can exaggerate it sometimes, but there is a Cologne mentality, which I like. It's about comfort, hospitality and friendliness. In Cologne, anyone can join in and nobody is rejected,' he says.

Where other Germans are more reserved, Kölners and Rhinelanders pride themselves on their joie de vivre and emotional openness. 'Maybe it's a Catholic thing. In Catholicism, you can always just confess to all your sins and be absolved, so maybe it's easier to be a bit more laissez-faire.' jokes Niedecken, who describes himself as 'a residual Catholic, like most people in Cologne'. Even if the city is less defined by religion than it once was, he notes, the *Dom* still looms large both physically and culturally. Yet he also sees another reason for Cologne's openness. 'We have the Rhine, and the Rhine was a trade route. In the Middle Ages, foreigners who sailed their goods down the river were obliged to stop in Cologne to sell them, and anyone who wanted to cross the Rhine would have to come to Cologne to go over the bridge. That made this city a marketplace, where people from all over met each other and learned to get along.'

Nowadays, Cologne is known as one of the most progressive and tolerant cities in Germany. In 2023, it was ranked as the most sexually liberal city in the world by *Lust* magazine, ahead of both Amsterdam and Berlin. And while it might be a stretch to draw a direct line from its trading history to its current liberalism, both play a role in the city's footballing identity. The iconic towers at Köln's RheinEnergie-Stadion are designed as an homage to the bridges over the Rhine, and Cologne's ultras are known for having a strong progressive streak. 'I remember one game where the away block started singing, "You are the capital of the gays", and our ultras just turned it around and sang, "We are the capital of the gays!" That was fantastic,' says Niedecken.

His own music was always cut from a similar cloth. From their searing anti-fascist hit *'Kristallnaach'* in 1982 to their performance at a protest against nuclear weapons at the NATO summit in Bonn in the same year, BAP always leaned more towards the left-wing, progressive side of German politics. Their 'Kölschrock' may partly be an exercise in cultural conservation, but it is a far cry from the social conservatism of the Catholic bishops or Konrad Adenauer's CDU. Instead, Niedecken and his peers belonged to a generation who, in their ferocious pursuit of social change, would push through the next phase of West Germany's development into a modern, liberal society. As the newly formed Bundesliga transformed German football from the 1960s onwards, the country's political and popular culture were also going through a major transformation. The revolution had arrived, and the young people were taking power.

When Hennes the goat first strolled up the touchline in Cologne in 1950, his namesake was still at the very beginning of an illustrious managerial career. As he oversaw Köln's rise to prominence during two spells in charge in the 1950s, Hennes Weisweiler quickly established himself as one of Germany's best young coaches. In 1954, he was briefly enlisted as assistant to Germany boss Sepp Herberger after the World Cup win. A decade later in 1964, it was Herberger who recommended Weisweiler to the directors of a small, ambitious Rhineland club called Borussia Mönchengladbach. The move would define Weisweiler's career, turn Gladbach into one of the biggest clubs in the country, and transform the national game forever.

Things were changing anyway in the 1960s. Konrad Adenauer left office in 1963, and his patrician politics were falling out of fashion. By the end of the decade, his CDU party would be replaced by the first centre-left government of the post-war era. Under social-democratic Chancellor Willy Brandt, West German foreign policy shifted and the country took a more conciliatory approach to the GDR and the Soviet Union. At the same time, Germans' relationship to their Nazi past began to change. For all his achievements in making the Federal Republic a functioning democracy, Adenauer had taken a soft-handed approach to denazification, allowing many high-ranking Nazis, including his own long-time chief of staff Hans Globke, to remain in positions of influence after the war. 'There's no point throwing out dirty water if you don't have any clean,' he purportedly told journalists in 1952. By the mid-1960s, however, the high-profile Auschwitz trials in Frankfurt had brought debates about the Holocaust into the centre of society, and a new generation of West German students was demanding more accountability from their own country. The 'sixty-eighters', as the generation became known, would have a lasting effect on German politics.

As the student protests reached their furious peak in the summer of 1968, two football teams were also emerging who would come to dominate the German game over the following decade. In the 1968/9 season, a young Bayern Munich side led by captain Franz Beckenbauer won their first ever title of the Bundesliga era. A year later in 1970, Weisweiler's Borussia Mönchengladbach became German champions for the very first time. Over the following years, these two groups of players transformed club football and led West Germany to glory at the 1972 European Championships and the 1974 World Cup. In doing so, they would come to be seen as the footballing embodiment of the revolutionary sixty-eighter generation. 'They were more confident than the previous generation of players,' the French-German politician and former student leader Daniel Cohn-Bendit told *Kicker* magazine in 2022. 'They showed that they would decide themselves how they wanted to play, and that was like a mirror image to our [social] upheaval.'

Gladbach in particular were seen as footballing revolutionaries. 'We weren't called the Foals for nothing,' says former midfield star Rainer Bonhof, who joined the club as a seventeen-year-old in 1970. The nickname 'Foals' had been coined before his arrival due to the team's high proportion of young players, and it soon became synonymous with their exhilarating style of play under Weisweiler. 'We played this heart-racing football, which people weren't used to at the time. Bayern were different, they would go 2–0 up and then defend the lead. With us, 2–0 wouldn't be enough, we'd just keep on attacking, and people took to that. On the one hand, you had this pragmatic football, and on the other you had these pulse-racing Foals.'

It is a narrative that has long since established itself in the mythology of German football: Bayern as the efficient, powerful establishment machine and Gladbach as the footballing sixty-eighters, the swashbuckling rebels. As football writer Uli Hesse points out in his book *Tor!*, it is not one that stands up to much scrutiny. Bayern also played attacking football and with their five league titles and one UEFA Cup, Gladbach were at least as efficient in collecting silverware. Yet the idea stuck, and there were reasons for that.

The first was Weisweiler. In his decade in charge of Gladbach, the Rhinelander proved himself as one of the great coaching pioneers of German football. One of the first clubs to introduce a dedicated fitness coach, Borussia's relentlessly energetic style would leave a legacy which coaches like Jürgen Klopp would still be drawing on decades later. As Bonhof says, they kept coming at you regardless of the scoreline, and they are still responsible for several of the highest wins in Bundesliga history, including an 11–0 drubbing of Schalke in 1967. The limits of Weisweiler's style would later be exposed in an unhappy season at Barcelona, but Bonhof insists he was still revolutionary in the development of attacking football. 'I do think he played a leading role in the changes that were happening then. He was a perfectionist and he demanded everything of you. That was good for us, good for the club, and it was good for the city and the region,' he says.

Borussia certainly put Mönchengladbach on the map, which may be another reason why they were seen as the more likeable alternative to Bayern. Though once known as the

'Manchester of the Rhineland' for its thriving textile industry, Mönchengladbach was never a major centre and its population was around a tenth the size of Munich's in the 1970s. While Bayern played in their city's huge, modern Olympiastadion from 1972, Borussia had the Bökelbergstadion, a small, old-fashioned terraced ground squeezed between residential streets on the site of an old gravel pit. In an era when most German clubs played in huge, cavernous arenas with running tracks, the cramped, football-only Bökelberg had an air of anarchy to it. In 1971, a Bundesliga game there was abandoned after one of the goalposts collapsed. Later that year, a 7–1 win over Inter Milan in the European Cup was declared null and void after Inter's Roberto Boninsegna was apparently hit by a cola can thrown from the stands. To this day, many Gladbach fans insist that Boninsegna was faking and they were robbed. Either way, the Bökelberg was not a welcoming place for opposition players. 'You were so close to the fans, you could feel all the emotions,' says Bonhof. 'It was a fortress, a perfect paddock for eleven hungry young Foals.'

Above all, though, the link between Gladbach and the sixty-eighter generation centred around one young Foal in particular. Günter Netzer was Borussia's playmaker under Weisweiler, and with his long hair and extravagant lifestyle, he was also Germany's first rock'n'roll footballer. While Bayern had the clean-cut 'Kaiser' Franz Beckenbauer as their on-field leader, Gladbach had Netzer, a man who ran a nightclub in the city centre and turned up to training in a Jaguar. 'Günter had a reputation. He was completely normal in the dressing room, but he also did things that were completely unusual for a footballer at the time,' says Bonhof. He also repeatedly clashed with

Weisweiler, further fuelling his rebel image. 'I was completely unpolitical,' Netzer told the *Stuttgarter Nachrichten* newspaper in 2014. 'But the sixty-eighters saw me as someone who embodied their values by brushing up against authority.' The most famous act of brilliant defiance came in 1973, when he substituted himself on in the cup final against Cologne and immediately scored the winning goal.

That game was Netzer's last for Gladbach. He left for Real Madrid later that summer, becoming one of the first German players to achieve stardom abroad. Gladbach would go on to win three more league titles without him, but when Weisweiler left for Barcelona in 1976, it was the beginning of the end for the Foals. By the time the great coach returned to Germany and won the double with his hometown club Köln in 1978, the glory years were over in Mönchengladbach. Just like many of the student activists of 1968, most of the original Foals soon became part of the establishment. Netzer had success as sporting director at Hamburg before spending many years as a pundit. Berti Vogts and Jupp Heynckes both became successful managers at home and abroad. Bonhof himself has been Borussia's vice-president since 2009.

The club he presides over is now very different to the one he played for back in the 1970s. Gladbach moved out of the Bökelberg in 2006, and the iconic old stadium is now little more than a memorial site. Though they are partially covered by a housing development, you can still trace the shape of the old uncovered stands. The terraces have been landscaped into grassy banks, and on the footpath which snakes around the edge of the pitch, signs remind residents to keep their dogs on the lead. It is quiet, suburban, and not a place that screams of revolution.' The new ground, Borussia-Park, is a different beast entirely. Another one of the many new grounds built in the lead-up to the 2006 World Cup, it is a paint-by-numbers modern football stadium a half-hour bus ride out of town, complete with extensive training facilities, enormous car parks and an on-site hotel.

'Keep dogs on the lead': Gladbach's famous Bökelbergstadion has now been transformed into a housing estate. © Kit Holden

It is a ground that is undoubtedly more suited to a club of Borussia's size. Incredibly for a town of just 250,000 inhabitants, Gladbach still sell more than 50,000 tickets for most home games. They remain the sixth-largest football club in Germany by number of members, and still enjoy huge popularity across the country, especially among football intellectuals of a certain age. They are also still very much the pride of their own town. As Bonhof says, that is the legacy of the wild early years of the legendary Foals. 'Everyone in this city, from the butcher to the baker to the postman, is a Borussia fan. That's something we started in the 1960s and 1970s, and has endured to this day,' he says.

Yet there is also a good reason why Mönchengladbach was not selected as a host city for Euro 2024. After all, an out-of-town arena in a city with limited transport links is not the best place to hold major tournament games. Especially when there is a similar-sized stadium right in the middle of a much bigger city. For all their lasting glamour, Gladbach remain a big club in a small town. At Fortuna Düsseldorf, the Rhineland's third great club, they have the opposite problem.

Nowadays, there is little love lost between Borussia Mönchengladbach and 1. FC Köln. The pair are bitter rivals on opposing sides of the so-called Rhine derby, but as Rainer Bonhof points out, it wasn't always so. Hennes Weisweiler was always revered in both cities, and Bonhof himself ended his career in Cologne after a brief spell at Valencia. Traditionally, Köln's biggest rivalry was not with Mönchengladbach. Nor was it with their nearest neighbours, Bayer Leverkusen, the club of the local pharmaceuticals giant who rose to prominence in the 1980s and 1990s. The Rhine rivalry that really mattered was always with the only city that could match Cologne for size and influence in the region: Düsseldorf.

Only forty kilometres separate the Rhineland's two biggest cities, but anyone from either of them will tell you that Cologne and Düsseldorf are chalk and cheese. Legend has it that the animosity between the two cities goes back to the thirteenth century, but in reality, this is a modern feud. As Germany industrialised in the nineteenth century and Düsseldorf became a new hub for banking and trade, Cologne's economic hegemony on the Rhine was suddenly threatened. Since then, the two cities have spat tacks at each other from their respective sides of the river. On the right bank to the north: the well-dressed nouveau-riche of modern Düsseldorf. On the left bank further south: the god-fearing bon vivants of Roman Cologne.

Cologne is larger, but Düsseldorf far outstrips it on GDP per capita and is the state capital of North Rhine-Westphalia. The two cities often compete over the region's infrastructure and prestige institutions, and they love nothing more than a squabble over trivialities. Carnival revellers say *Helau* in Düsseldorf and *Alaaf* in Cologne, and using the wrong greeting in the wrong town will get you short shrift. Beer, naturally, is also a bone of contention. Cologne prefers the light, lagerish *Kölsch*, which is served in dainty, thin glasses carried in huge wooden wreaths. Düsseldorf goes for the richer, darker *Alt*, which comes in a slightly stouter vessel. Both cities insist their style is superior. A study in 2016 subjected fifty men from each city to a blindfolded taste test and found that none of them could tell the difference.

And then there is football. Historically speaking, Fortuna Düsseldorf is a name with just as much gravitas as that of 1. FC Köln. Fortuna were one of the first clubs from western Germany to be crowned national champions, and the club's hall of fame includes national icons like World Cup winning goalkeeper Toni Turek and European Championship winning manager Jupp Derwall. After Gladbach's four league titles and Köln's domestic double in 1978, Fortuna Düsseldorf crowned a decade of Rhenish success by winning back-to-back German Cups in 1979 and 1980. They beat Köln in the second of the two finals, ensuring beyond any doubt that the age-old city rivalry now also extended to football. But whereas the debates over beer and Carnival may never be settled, the question of on-field supremacy has long been clear cut. Both clubs have had their ups and downs in recent decades. Cologne have tended to ride out the storms and keep returning to the top flight. Fortuna have proven less fortunate.

The two cup wins remain the height of Düsseldorf's footballing success in the modern era. After a sixteen-year stretch in the Bundesliga, Fortuna began to tumble down the divisions from the mid-1980s onwards, eventually ending up on the brink of collapse in the fourth tier. In 2001, they avoided bankruptcy only thanks to the intervention of their celebrity fans, with punk rock band Die Toten Hosen stepping in to bail the club out financially. The band's singer, Campino, is also a Liverpool fan and a friend of Jürgen Klopp's. 'I'm trying to persuade Jürgen to try his luck with a second-division club,' he joked in an interview with the *Rheinische Post* in 2023.

For now, though, Fortuna remain a yo-yo club, wandering between the top two divisions with little hope of recovering their old glamour. On the rare occasion they do get promoted, relegation tends to follow swiftly. If Cologne are the Carnival club, Düsseldorf are the experts in purgatory. Or as Campino himself once put it: 'Everyone has to believe in something, even if it's Fortuna Düsseldorf.'

It is, perhaps, not all that surprising that Fortuna are not among German football's big hitters. For one thing, Düsseldorf is not a typical football city. The club may have working-class roots, but the town itself is known as much for its haute cuisine and high-end retailers as its gritty industrialism. Düsseldorf, they say, is a city which doesn't really know what it is: an industrial centre and former royal residence which is known for both shipping and shopping. Its football fans are equally hard to pin down. On the one hand, Fortuna are one of the most famous clubs in Germany, and the only team in their town. At times, it seems every bar, kebab joint and tobacconist in Düsseldorf has a Fortuna scarf over the door. Yet for all that, the club remains curiously under-supported. Unlike Cologne and Gladbach, who fill their stadium every week, Fortuna have always had problems getting bums on seats.

That is at least partly down to simple bad timing. Whereas Köln and Gladbach became big in the golden era of German football, Fortuna hit their heights in the late 1970s and early 1980s, when the game was beginning to take a downward turn. As in other countries, football endured a mini dark ages in Germany in the 1980s, with dwindling spectator numbers and increasing levels of violence on the terraces. Despite being the only major club in Germany's seventh-largest city and having recently reached three domestic and one European Cup final, Fortuna failed to draw crowds much above 10,000 in the early 1980s. When the Annual Conference of the Catholic Church brought 50,000 people to the Rheinstadion in 1982, Fortuna's then president, Werner Faßbender, couldn't resist a joke. 'We should have locked the doors and kept them all in there until the game against Hamburg,' he quipped.

The old Rheinstadion was torn down in the 2000s, and the new arena which replaced it was supposed to usher in a new era for Düsseldorf. In some ways, it has. The Düsseldorf Arena is one of the biggest and most accessible of Germany's modern grounds, and, unlike Mönchengladbach, it was a safe pick as a host city for Euro 2024. Yet it is not a ground that stirs the emotions. From the outside, it looks identical to the multi-storey car park next door. And now as ever, Fortuna struggle to fill it. At most second-division games, around a third of the 50,000 seats remain empty. In a country where attendances are generally higher than almost everywhere else in Europe, that is a remarkably low rate of attendance.

In April 2023, the club announced radical steps to rectify that situation. Under the tagline 'Fortuna for all', they revealed a new plan to provide free entry to all spectators, with sponsors and commercial partners making up the lost ticket revenue. The programme, which was trialled at selected games in the 2023/24 season, was the first of its kind in professional men's football in Germany. Its architects presented it as a democratic revolution which would breathe new life into Fortuna. Germany's ever-critical fan groups were more sceptical, arguing that allowing sponsors to pay for fans was simply commercialisation by another means. Rather than empower the stadium-going supporter, critics argued, it would make them the recipients of commercial charity, thereby disenfranchising them further. Yet whichever side one took, the plan was undoubtedly, on some level, an admission of defeat. Despite their proud history, modern infrastructure, and lack of any significant city rival, Fortuna simply don't have the pulling power to fill a stadium with traditional ticket sales. 'Fortuna belongs to Düsseldorf like the Rhine or Altbier,' said Campino in 2001. Yet in the Rhineland, they continue to play third fiddle to footballing royalty like Cologne and Gladbach.

Even in those cities, though, the shine of the Rhine is not what it once was. If clubs like Cologne and Gladbach were brimming with the spirit of the age in the mid-twentieth century, the zeitgeist has now long since moved on. Since reunification, the balance of political power in Germany has naturally shifted away from its former western heartland. In 1991, the German parliament voted narrowly to move the seat of government from Bonn to Berlin, a process which was completed in 1999. North Rhine-Westphalia is still Germany's most populous state and has produced several of its most influential modern politicians, including former European Parliament president Martin Schulz, current CDU leader Friedrich Merz and finance minister Christian Lindner. But broadly speaking, the Federal Republic is no longer a country that is shaped on the banks of the Rhine. In football, too, it is no longer the superpower it once was. When Bayer Leverkusen won their first ever league title in 2024, they were the first Rhineland club to win a major trophy in thirty years. While Cologne and Gladbach still attract big crowds, the days when people expected them to dominate the national game are long gone.

THE RHINELAND

Just a short way up the road, things are different. North of Düsseldorf, Carnival country begins to fade as the rolling hills of the Rhineland give way into the former coal mines and steelworks of the Ruhr region. And there, in the grey streets of cities like Dortmund, Essen, Gelsenkirchen and Bochum, football matters just that little bit more.

THE RUHR

GELSENKIRCHEN
DORTMUND

3
THE RUHR
HEART AND COAL

The Church of the Holy Trinity is full and everyone is wearing black and yellow. It is the day before the final game of the 2022/23 Bundesliga season, and the Borussia Dortmund fans have come to make one final plea to the powers on high. Their team need just one more win to clinch a ninth German title, and where better to pray for that win than here, in a church just two blocks up from where the club was founded? As the organ strikes up the first chord, the congregation raise their scarves and launch into a full-blooded chorus of 'You'll Never Walk Alone'. Later, as they leave the church, they will murmur the prayer inscribed at the back of the nave to the left of the Virgin Mary: 'God the Father, the Son and the Holy Spirit, we entrust to you the fortunes of our football club, Borussia Dortmund, its players, directors and fans...'

Welcome to the Ruhr, where football is a religion.

Fifteen miles away in Gelsenkirchen, there is another church. This one, St. Joseph's, is on the corner of a crossroads in Schalke, the district that was once the heart of the city's coal-mining industry. Like its counterpart in Dortmund, it too is a place of football devotion, but this time kitted out in the blue and white of FC Schalke 04. In one of the stained-glass windows St. Aloysius stands in a field of lilies with a halo around his head and a cross clasped tightly in his left hand. Look more closely, and you see he is also wearing football boots and has a blue and white leather ball at his feet. Around here, you can't not be a Schalke fan. Even if you are a sixteenth-century Italian Jesuit.

This is how things work in the Ruhr, the cluster of smokestack cities that make up Germany's former industrial heartland. Named after the river which snakes from east to west before joining the Rhine at Duisburg, the Ruhr's coal and steel industries kept Germany running for 150 years. For much of that time, they also attracted jobseekers from across the German-speaking world and beyond. Known colloquially as the *Ruhrpott*, the region has always been a melting pot of confessions, cultures and creeds. But if there is one thing they all believe in, it is football.

As in other industrial regions across Europe, football found fertile ground in the Ruhr's red soil, and the region has long been considered the spiritual home of football in Germany. An area not much bigger than Norfolk or Rhode Island, it has always been disproportionately successful on the pitch. The first clubs here emerged in the early twentieth century, just as the Ruhr was being transformed from a rural backwater into an industrial centre. In the 1930s, when its coal and steel were feeding the Nazi war machine, Schalke dominated the national game. In the 1950s, as the Ruhr's productivity helped fuel West Germany's economic miracle and build lasting peace, Borussia Dortmund and Rot-Weiss Essen joined the party. In total, seven teams from the Ruhr have played in the Bundesliga, and the region can boast

At St. Joseph's Church in Gelsenkirchen, St. Aloysius is depicted as a football-playing Schalke fan. © Olivier Kruschinski

sixteen national titles and eleven DFB-Pokal wins. Nowhere else in Germany are there so many iconic clubs in such a small space, and nowhere else is football so intimately entwined with the history and identity of the region.

As the old industries crumbled in the second half of the century, the Ruhr's footballing power also began to wane, and some of its clubs never recovered. The once mighty MSV Duisburg have sunk into third-tier mediocrity, while SG Wattenscheid and Rot-Weiss Oberhausen have plummeted even further. Perhaps the biggest fallen giant of all is Rot-Weiss Essen, the 1955 German champions whose city once boasted the largest coal mine in Europe. The Zollverein mine closed in 1986 and is now a UNESCO World Heritage Site. Rot-Weiss were relegated from the Bundesliga in 1977, never to return.

Yet even long after the region's golden age, two clubs have kept the flame of the Ruhr alive. Borussia Dortmund are one of only three German teams to have won the European Cup and, for most of the twenty-first century, have been German football's second major power behind Bayern Munich. Their world-famous stadium can hold 80,000 people, more than a quarter of whom stand on the fearsome 'Yellow Wall', Europe's largest standing terrace. Their arch-rivals, Schalke, meanwhile, can boast almost as many members, a UEFA Cup title, and a youth academy which has produced players like Manuel Neuer, Leroy Sané and Mesut Özil. In a region of countless local rivalries, this is the big one. The Ruhr derby, or *Revierderby*, is still German football's biggest grudge match.

Dortmund and Schalke have more in common than they care to admit. Both started as working-class neighbourhood clubs and are now global brands, far more famous than their respective cities. Both remain the cultural lifeblood of their respective cities.

In Dortmund and Gelsenkirchen, their colours are everywhere, from the bars and the stadiums right into the museums, the town halls and even the churches. Like all cities in the Ruhr, these two have also struggled with deindustrialisation, facing mass unemployment and the socio-political problems that come with it. But Dortmund has Ballspielverein Borussia – or 'BVB' – and Gelsenkirchen has Schalke. And at the very least, that has kept the pride of the Ruhr alive.

In recent years, the fortunes of Dortmund and Schalke have begun to diverge. BVB continue to challenge for silverware and are now one of the most successful football clubs in the world, while Schalke are stuck in a vicious circle of crisis and decline. And in different ways, that puts both clubs in an identity crisis. In places like the Ruhr, football matters so much because it provides a link to a more secure, more prosperous time. It offers a sense of community and identity in a world where many of the old certainties have long since crumbled. But for the clubs themselves, that can be both a blessing and a curse.

Olivier Kruschinski insists he is not a Schalke fan. 'I'm a *Schalker*,' he says. 'It's different. You don't become a *Schalker*, you are one. Grandpa. Dad. Me. That's how it is.'

Kruschinski's grandfather was a coal miner in Gelsenkirchen. Had he been born into a different generation, he too would probably have been down the mines from the age of fourteen. As it is, Kruschinski is a Schalker mainly in the footballing sense. But as he explains, football in Schalke is inextricable from its history as a mining district. 'Nowhere else in Germany do people live and breathe football like they do here, and that has everything to do with the history of the city,' says Kruschinski. 'Football was an exit strategy, a chance to break out of the mining life. It gave people courage, optimism and self-worth in an otherwise sad, monotone and highly mechanised day-to-day.'

Schalke the district was built to house the miners who worked at the nearby 'Consolidation' mine. At its height, the *Consol* was one of the biggest coal mines in the whole of the Ruhr, employing almost six thousand people and shifting millions of tons of black gold a year. It was also the motor of Gelsenkirchen's economy: the main furnace in the 'city of a thousand fires'. Schalke the club was also born of the mine. It was founded by Consol apprentices in 1904, and the mine would go on to support it financially for years to come, even providing the land for Schalke's first stadium: the Kampfbahn Glückauf. A number of the club's earliest superstars, including the great striker Ernst Kuzorra, also worked down the Consol, and Schalke's identity has remained inseparable from coal even after the mine shut in 1993. Still today, football commentators and fans talk about being 'on Schalke' rather than 'in' or 'at' Schalke, an affectation borrowed from mining vernacular.

Kruschinski has been a Schalker all his life, and he knows both the district and the club inside out. On matchdays, he runs football-themed walking tours around the area's streets and landmarks. They are wildly successful, with home and away fans alike turning up in their dozens every fortnight. He takes fans to what he calls the 'iconic' places of Schalke's history, but he admits they are not much to look at. The Kampfbahn Glückauf stadium, where the club played from 1928 to 1972, now has grassy banks instead of terraces, and its artificial pitch is used only by local amateur teams. The Schalker Markt, a central square where the club was founded and superstar Kuzorra ran a tobacco shop, is now just a car park. The Schalker Straße, which Kruschinski says was once the most glamorous shopping street in western Germany, is today a quiet, unassuming row of mid-century new builds. War damage and post-industrial decline have ravaged Gelsenkirchen and it has a reputation as an unhappy place. The unemployment rate here is the highest in Germany and has remained steady at around fourteen per cent – double the national average – for most of this century.[3]

The story Kruschinski tells on his tours, however, attempts to challenge some of the established narratives. He starts by talking about the beginnings of industrialisation, when the Ruhr was transformed from a sleepy agrarian stretch of land just north of Düsseldorf to a place of revolution and flux on the cutting edge of technological progress. The mining industry was originally built on innovation, he argues, casting the coal barons as the 'Zuckerbergs of their day' and the Ruhr as 'Silicon Valley'. The people who worked there created an entirely new community, one whose roots and identity were firmly tied up with the modernity of their work.

The Ruhr has always been a place of immigration, where people came to find work from other parts of Germany and beyond. 'My name is Olivier Kruschinski, I am a French Polack,' he says to nervous titters at one point in the tour. Polish names like Kruschinski and Kuzorra are a relic of the early twentieth century, when thousands of workers moved to the Ruhr from Polish-speaking Masuria, which was then part of the German Empire. That was one of the first waves of immigration that changed the region, but was by no means the last. After the Second World War, the Ruhr also welcomed many Germans who had fled persecution in the east, as well as thousands who came from abroad to work in West Germany. In the 1950s and 1960s, the Federal Republic signed labour agreements with countries like Turkey, Greece and Italy to bring much-needed manpower to the booming post-war economy. Many of these so-called *Gastarbeiter*, or 'guest workers', settled and Germany is still home to the largest Turkish diaspora in Europe. There are an estimated 1.5 million Turkish citizens living in Germany, and another 1.5 million German citizens who have either dual citizenship or family roots in Turkey.[4] Though the diaspora is spread across the country, it is the Ruhr which has produced its most famous footballers. Both Ilkay Gündogan and Mesut Özil are Germans of Turkish descent, born in Gelsenkirchen.

The story of immigration in the Ruhr has not always been a happy one, and both the Masurian and the Turkish communities have faced racism and abuse over the years. Yet the region is also rightly proud of its multicultural identity, and Kruschinski argues football has played a role in that. As the Ruhr's population exploded at various points in the twentieth century, the game became an 'integration machine', second only to the workplace and the church, he says. 'You had millions of people coming together in a very short space of time and football was an easy way to project common visions and integrate more easily.' In other words, other parts of Germany already had their identities and traditions when football came along. In the Ruhr, identities were forged alongside, and in tandem with, the rise of football.

Perhaps the most famous archetype of Ruhr identity is the *Malocher*, the hard-grafting blue-collar manual labourer. Even now, Schalke fans love nothing more than a player who puts in the hard yards, grafting and scrapping for their club and their teammates like the miners of old. The legacy of those tireless migrant workers is, after all, still there today in people's names, their families and the way they talk. As Kruschinski explains, the direct, often coarse language of the Ruhr is also a hangover from the age of industry. When you work down the mines with people speaking many different dialects, you don't beat around the bush. 'What are these arseholes doing here?' Kruschinski says upon spotting two Werder Bremen fans at the back of his tour group. 'No offence, boys, I mean it in a nice way.'

Yet Kruschinski is keen to stress that there is more to Schalke's history than hard-working, rough-talking Malochers. As he says, mining was once cutting-edge technology and the first great Schalke team were also innovators, who changed the way football was played in Germany. Taking inspiration from British and Scottish teams and with Masurian superstars like Kuzorra and Fritz Szepan, they brought a brand-new style of play to Germany based on short passing rather than long punts forward. The so-called 'Schalker Kreisel', or spinning top style, left their opponents dizzy and ushered in the first great golden age of football in the Ruhr. Schalke won six titles between 1934 and 1942, putting the region on the football map.

The fact that Schalke's golden age coincided with the rise of Nazism is largely coincidence, yet the Ruhr itself was undoubtedly central to Hitler's designs for Germany and Europe. When the Nazis rose to power in the early 1930s, they did so with the support of wealthy Ruhr industrialists like the steel magnate Fritz Thyssen, and the coal mines would go on to fuel the regime's massively accelerated rearmament drive in the years that followed. The Ruhr, accordingly, was not spared the horrors of what was to follow. During the war itself, as more and more of the miners and steelworkers were called up to serve in the military, its industry was kept going in part by domestic and foreign forced labour. The strategic importance of industrial cities like Gelsenkirchen also meant they were subjected to heavy bombing. By the end of the war, vast swathes of the town were destroyed and the Ruhr economy was briefly brought to its knees. In 1945, Schalke and other football teams earned their keep with so-called 'potato games', touring the local villages to play matches in return for food and supplies.

The ground beneath them was still full of black gold, however, and the Ruhr would soon prove instrumental in driving the economic miracle that stabilised democratic West Germany after the war. In the 1950s, its football clubs picked up from where the once dominant Schalke had left off. In 1954, Rot-Weiss Essen striker Helmut Rahn scored the winner as West Germany won the World Cup final in Switzerland. A year later, Essen won the German championship, before passing the baton to Ruhr neighbours Dortmund in 1956 and 1957. Schalke cemented the region's hegemony a year later with their seventh title. At that point, nobody could have known it would be their last.

But by the late 1950s, the walls were beginning to close in on both district and club. The coal crisis saw the end of subventions and the first mine closures in 1959, which started a long process of decline. The rise of oil and nuclear power, as well as the increase in cheaper coal outside of Germany, slowly but surely chipped away at coal's significance. Schalke would never again reach their dizzying pre-war heights, and as the decades ground on, they became increasingly reliant on support from the local authorities and external sponsors, rather than their traditional local industrialist backers. The Consolidation mine had been the city's lifeblood, and there was no industry able to fill the enormous boots of the declining coal sector. As the last mines closed in the 1990s and 2000s, all Gelsenkirchen had left was Schalke 04, and the stories of its glorious industrial past.

'As soon as the coal era ended, people started to romanticise it,' explains Kruschinski. 'That's normal. It's just what people do, and it's justified to a certain extent because the coal industry here had such a huge influence on the economic power of the whole country.' Everywhere, from the photos of old mines in the train station to the St. Joseph's church, the coal industry is lionised, romanticised, exalted. In recent decades, Schalke have bought even further in to their history as a miners' club, making it a central part of their brand identity. The club shop sells branded t-shirts with pictures of coal-covered workers and the crossed hammer and chisel symbol. Even the players' tunnel at the Veltins Arena has been decorated to look like the inside of a coal mine. Every fortnight, when the players walk out onto the pitch, the whole stadium greets them with the 'Steigerlied', a traditional mining song.

Kruschinski calls it an identity trap: 'We should be brave and visionary in the way we think about our city. But too often, we get stuck in these legends of the hardworking Malocher,' he says. It is not that he isn't extremely proud of his town's history, but he insists that the obsession with the punishing and life-threatening work of his forefathers can be counterproductive. 'At the end of the day, there's a reason why nobody now wants to work like a pig all day in inhumane conditions down a mine. If it's so good, why isn't everyone moving to Turkey where there is still a mining industry? I don't want to say it was all negative either, but it can sometimes be a bit too much.' The point of his tours is not just to keep the memory of the past alive, but also to find new narratives and new threads which the city can pick up going forward. 'It seems unlikely that we're ever going to get a new coal mine or a new steel works here. We need to get together and write a new story.'

Coal, after all, has not been an actual part of daily life for a generation. 'When I go abroad, people don't know Gelsenkirchen as a mining town. They know that it's the city of Ilkay Gündogan and Manuel Neuer,' says Kruschinski. Those modern-day superstars, as well as the tactical innovations of the great Schalker Kreisel teams, are as much a part of the city's heritage as the mines, he argues. Most Schalke fans, meanwhile, have never worked a day down a mine in their lives, and the club's success in the early twenty-first century was built not on local coal, but on Russian gas. For seventeen years, Schalke were sponsored by the Russian state-owned gas company Gazprom, until they finally cut ties over the full-scale invasion of Ukraine in 2022. For a long time, the deal kept Schalke in the big time, yet it also proved to be a poisoned chalice. The political fallout only deepened the divisions within the club, arguably hastening Schalke's decline in the late 2010s and early 2020s. Kruschinski lets out a long sigh when he talks about it. 'Being self-critical is a typical Schalker trait, and that's a good thing. But we do have a tendency to talk ourselves down and tear ourselves apart,' he says.

By the time we finish the interview, we have crossed the entire city and arrived at the stadium. It is a few hours before Schalke kick-off in a crucial Bundesliga game against Werder Bremen, and as 62,000 fans swarm through the gates, it feels like the whole city is here. These days, Schalke are fighting to stay in the league rather than win it, but they remain one of the biggest clubs in the country. On matchday, Gelsenkirchen still burns with furious, intransigent pride. Perhaps, on some levels, that is enough to keep a city going after coal.

Yet football is not always balm for the soul. Most modern Schalke fans have seen their team win trophies, but increasingly they have become more familiar with relegations, humiliations and gut-wrenching lows. In 2020, they went a whole year without a win. In 2001, they stormed the pitch thinking they had finally won the title, only to hear four minutes later that Bayern Munich had snatched it from under their noses. 'Schalke is like life. You can only enjoy the high points if you hit rock bottom every now and then. At this club, you're rejoicing to high heaven and plunged to the depths of despair in the space of a week,' says Kruschinski. Then he disappears into the stadium with the rest of the city.

Schalke beat Bremen, scoring two goals in the last ten minutes to come from behind and send a wave of ecstatic hope through Gelsenkirchen. Four weeks later, they are relegated.

Borsigplatz doesn't look like much. A small traffic interchange in the Nordstadt district of Dortmund, it is one of those places that could be anywhere in Germany. The roundabout is lined with trees, and in the buildings around the outside, there is a kebab shop, a few hairdressers and a handful of offices. It is pretty enough, but apart from the black-and-yellow flags fluttering from the lampposts, there is little sign that this is hallowed turf.

For Borussia Dortmund fans, however, Borsigplatz is a kind of Mecca, a place of pilgrimage spoken of only in hushed tones and with misty eyes. When Dortmund win a trophy, they always celebrate here, transforming the innocuous little square into a teeming sea of black and yellow. While some canny residents rent out their flats and balconies at astronomical prices, a Borsigplatz party is a religious experience for most Dortmund fans, a raucous community celebration that is a far cry from the sanitised world of commercial football. Jürgen Klopp admitted to weeping when he celebrated his first Bundesliga title there in 2011. He later confessed that he also got so drunk that he and club chairman Hans-Joachim Watzke woke up in the bus depot and had to hitchhike back home.

'We are party animals and we like nothing more than to celebrate here at Borsigplatz,' says Dortmund fan Annette Kritzler. Having lived near the square for more than thirty years, she has seen her fair share of title celebrations, and she knows the area better than most. Like Kruschinski, she runs football walking tours around the neighbourhood, and she too is fiercely proud of her home turf. Dortmund-Nordstadt has a reputation for high crime rates and social issues, but Kritzler insists the stereotypes don't do justice to what is a vibrant, tight-knit and multicultural community. Above all, it is a community that adores BVB. When Kritzler first arrived as a student in the 1990s, the local butcher told her in no uncertain terms that 'if you live around here, you are black and yellow'.

This, after all, is Borussia's birthplace. BVB's stadium may be on the other side of the city, but it was here, in the upstairs room of the Zum Wildschütz restaurant just a few blocks north of Borsigplatz, that the club was founded in 1909 and first given its iconic colours. Contrary to one old joke about 'black lungs and yellow teeth', there appears to be no particular reason why the original Borussia founders chose the colours they did. (Curiously enough, black and yellow are actually the official colours of the city of Munich, while Dortmund's official colours are red and white.) Yet as Kritzler points out, Dortmund's colours do reflect the

Borussia Dortmund players celebrate with fans at Borsigplatz after winning the DFB-Pokal in 2017. © Borussia Dortmund

city's industrial past. Unlike Gelsenkirchen, where coal reigned supreme, Dortmund had a slightly wider industrial base. 'We also had steel and breweries, so it makes sense that we play in the colours of iron and beer,' she says. The name 'Borussia' (neo-Latin for Prussia), was taken from one of the city's major breweries.

More than the beer, though, BVB were a club forged in Dortmund steel. Borsigplatz lay just a few blocks south of the Hoesch AG steelworks at Westfalenhütte, and the entire area was built to house the workers employed there. The Weiße Wiese stadium, where Borussia played from their founding until 1937, was on a recreation ground right next to the works, in what would later be renamed the Hoeschpark. 'Without Hoesch steel, this neighbourhood wouldn't exist, and without this neighbourhood, Borussia Dortmund wouldn't exist,' says Kritzler.

The club didn't always have the backing of the local community. In the early 1900s, so the story goes, the local chaplain at the Church of the Holy Trinity had banned his parishioners from playing football. Like much of the German establishment at the time, he considered the newly imported game unnatural, an 'English disease' which was harmful to the morality and constitution of young men. BVB's founder, a young steelworks official named Franz Jacobi, defied the ban, beginning a long local feud which escalated to the point of farce. According to one story, the players had to abandon a match before kick-off when they found that the priest had sawn their goalposts in half. Another tale has the two men coming to physical blows. In the film version, for which Kritzler was a researcher, the chaplain was even thrown down a flight of stairs. She admits that this may have been artistic licence.

Either way, Jacobi won in the end. The Church of the Holy Trinity is now a shrine to Borussia Dortmund, complete with a small exhibition on the club's history and regular football-themed services. The club also invests in community projects in the area, and on Borsigplatz itself, little Borussia banners hang from every lamppost. A few hundred metres down the road, a BVB-branded street football court sits beneath an enormous football mural at the former home of Dortmund legend Max Michallek. Borsigplatz is where the global brand BVB stays in touch with its industrial roots.

Yet just as in Gelsenkirchen, that past is increasingly becoming little more than an echo. The steel crisis hit Germany a few decades after the coal crisis, but it too transformed the Ruhr and its economy. The Hoesch company's steelworks at Westfalenhütte, which once employed thousands of people around Borsigplatz, has since been scaled down to a bare-bones operation and its blast furnaces sold off to China. 'People didn't just lose a workplace, they lost a part of their identity,' says Kritzler, and points out that other key local industries have also shrunk over the decades. 'We used to have at least eight breweries in Dortmund. Now it's only two. The beer still tastes OK, thank God, but we've also lost something there. And it's the same thing with coal.'

At the same time, Dortmund is a city that seems to exude a little more optimism than Gelsenkirchen. It undoubtedly has its problems – unemployment is high here too, and the city's western Dorstfeld district has a reputation as a neo-Nazi stronghold – but compared to other Ruhr cities, Dortmund has managed deindustrialisation relatively well, and now has a thriving services sector. The Hoesch steelworks at Westfalenhütte have been partly transformed into a logistics park. The old Union brewery, whose famous 'U' logo still dominates the Dortmund skyline, is now a cultural centre. 'We have definitely done well at pushing those structural changes in the right direction,' says Kritzler.

There are good reasons why some things may have worked better in Dortmund than elsewhere. First and foremost, the city had a more diverse industrial economy than its coal-heavy neighbours, which meant that when the crises came, they didn't all come at once. It is also older than many other towns in the Ruhr, having been a Hanseatic trading hub for centuries before industrialisation. It is still the largest centre in the historic region of Westphalia, meaning that it is better connected than other towns. And perhaps most importantly of all, it has Borussia.

For decades now, the shift in Dortmund's economy has gone hand in hand with the rise of BVB as a global brand. The local insurance company Continentale was also the club's shirt sponsor for much of the 1990s, while their competitors Signal Iduna now own the official naming rights for Dortmund's Westfalenstadion. Borussia's superstar players, meanwhile, tend to live on the shores of the Phoenixsee in the east of the city. An artificial lake built on the site of another former Hoesch steel plant, the spot is synonymous with the new post-industrial Dortmund.

In theory, these are all positive developments. If steel and coal are gone, it is better to replace them with something new. But Kritzler does worry that there is a social price attached to this shift. As well as the hard-working Malocher, she says, the other archetype of Ruhr identity was the *Kumpel* mentality, an unwavering loyalty and solidarity to one's neighbour which was borne out of the dangerous nature of industrial work. 'That used to be normal among working families. You stood by your family and your neighbours, because you'd be digging coal in the same mine,' says Kritzler. 'We don't have that in our work life anymore, so where do we get it from? How do we pass that mentality on to our children?'

Football can fill the gap to a certain extent. Just as at Schalke, Dortmund fans also love players who fit in to the regional archetypes of Malocher and Kumpel. Hardworking, down-to-earth local players like Marcel Schmelzer and Kevin Großkreutz still enjoy huge popularity at BVB, and Jürgen Klopp used to wear a cap with the word 'Pöhler' on it, a Ruhr term for street footballer. As at Schalke, there is a sense that everyone at BVB is careful to maintain something of the old Ruhr spirit. 'The industrial identity disappears, and football is what is left. Maybe you can build a new sense of identity and togetherness out of that,' says Kritzler.

Yet even in football, it is increasingly difficult to strike the balance between community and commerce. 'For a club to play at the highest level in this very capitalistic environment and still stay true to its roots in a working-class area is not easy,' says Kritzler.

Over the years, BVB have shifted their approach to that problem. In the 1990s, the club went on a radical commercialisation drive with the express intention of challenging Bayern Munich. They signed international stars like Julio Cesar da Silva and Paulo Sousa, and snapped up some of Germany's biggest talents in Matthias Sammer, Karl-Heinz Riedle and Andreas Möller. Money brought success, with Dortmund winning back-to-back league titles in 1995 and 1996 and the Champions League in 1997. In Bundesliga terms, this was turbo-capitalism, and as long as the trophies kept rolling in, people were happy. Yet the debts racked up. In 2000, BVB moved to free up funds by becoming the first ever German football club to float on the stock market.

It worked in the short term, but when the extent of the financial rot was exposed a few years later, the fans turned on president Gerd Niebaum. A new leadership was installed, and Dortmund pulled themselves back from the brink of bankruptcy. After restabilising, the club took a different tack. They spent more sustainably, focused on youth development, and carved out a niche for themselves as the likeable club among Europe's wealthy elite. This was a more wholesome form of football capitalism, a model of a megaclub with its feet on the ground and its heart in the right place. At the club's centenary in 2009, they unveiled a new motto: *Echte Liebe*. 'True love.'

The high watermark of this feel-good era came under Klopp. Strange as it seems from today's point of view, many BVB fans were sceptical when the floppy-haired coach arrived from Mainz in 2008. They were soon won over as he led Dortmund to two league titles, a German cup and a Champions League final in his seven years in charge. More importantly, perhaps, he revived the community spirit at a club that had outgrown itself in the previous decades. Despite not being from the Ruhr himself, Klopp brought the soul back into BVB, much as he would later do at Liverpool. Like all Dortmunders, Kritzler's eyes light up when she talks about him. 'Jürgen Klopp was such a down-to-earth, approachable person,' she says. 'He'd come to services at the Church of the Holy Trinity and talk to fans. His wife even did the Christmas reading one year. When he was here, it really felt like the *Echte Liebe* slogan rang true. But then it sort of fell apart after he left.'

She doesn't just mean the results. Dortmund have won the German Cup twice since Klopp's departure in 2015, but they have never quite managed to reconjure the spirit of his tenure. Without the feel-good factor in the dugout, things like rising ticket prices or sweatshop-produced club merchandise have been harder to swallow. At times, it has felt like the old gap between the club's local roots and its brand has become wider and wider. Though their club continues to challenge for the Bundesliga title and play regularly in the Champions League, many Dortmund fans wonder whether success can really replace the sense of community and shared history that makes football in the Ruhr so special.

As Kritzler puts it: 'We talk about true love, but the question is: true love for what exactly?'

On 27 May 2023, the city of Dortmund suffered one of the biggest heartbreaks in its history. It was the final day of the Bundesliga season, and BVB were on the brink of a first Bundesliga title in eleven years. Two points adrift at the top of the table, they needed just one more victory to be crowned champions and end

Bayern Munich's decade of dominance. Instead, they slumped to a 2–2 draw at home to mid-table Mainz, throwing away the title in the most dramatic fashion. At full time, as disbelieving Bayern players celebrated a few miles down the road in Cologne, the entire Dortmund team stood in the penalty area like a routed army. Some of them stared into space. Others pulled their shirts over their eyes. Edin Terzic, Borussia's Dortmund-born head coach, wept before of the cameras. In front of them the famous Yellow Wall stood silent.

'Silence was the only suitable reaction,' says former Dortmund striker and current youth academy director Lars Ricken. It is a few days after the disaster, and Ricken is sitting in his office at the club's headquarters, a state-of-the-art modern complex on the site of an old British Royal Air Force base. It is a hot day, the air is still, and Dortmund still feels like a city in shock. It is as if they can still hear it: the echo of that crushing, heart-stopping silence of Saturday afternoon. 'We can be the loudest stadium in the world and we can also be the quietest,' says Ricken with a grimace.

If there is one place in Dortmund that means more to BVB fans than Borsigplatz, then it is the stadium. The 80,000-capacity arena in the south of the city is a monster, the largest football ground in Germany and the sixth largest in Europe. It dwarfs the Kampfbahn Rote Erde next door, which was Borussia's home until 1974. When the new ground was built for that year's World Cup, it was a novelty: a rare football-only stadium at a time when most German arenas had a running track. As it has expanded over the years, its cult status has only grown. Nowadays, it is the biggest building in the Dortmund skyline, the huge yellow pylons on its roof recognisable for miles around. Its official title is Signal Iduna Park and at Euro 2024 it will be branded as 'BVB Stadion

The famous 'Yellow Wall' can hold almost 25,000 fans in one stand. © Borussia Dortmund

Dortmund'. But its traditional name is Westfalenstadion, and the BVB fans refer to it simply as 'the temple'.

The temple's altar is the *Südtribüne*, the enormous stand at the south end of the stadium where the Dortmund ultras lead the support on matchdays. It is known the world over as the 'Yellow Wall', but it is really more of a cliff face, which rises unrelenting behind the goal, daring the players below to take it on. Around 25,000 people can fit onto its standing terraces: a whole stadium's worth packed into one single-tier block. On matchdays, it is a furious ocean of noise and yellow flags. At its best, it is also a weapon, able to intimidate even the best opposition and turn a game by sheer force of will.

It is also Borussia Dortmund in a nutshell. On the one hand, the Westfalenstadion is a genuinely spiritual place. At times like May 2023, when 80,000 people stood silently in collective shock, it can seem to be the very soul of the Ruhr, a medium for all the region's hopes, dreams, fears and regrets. On the other hand, it is also the iconic symbol of an international brand, a global byword for German fan culture, and a bucket-list tourist destination for groundhoppers across the world. This is the St. Peter's Basilica of German football, the Taj Mahal of the Bundesliga. A place always caught between its deep significance to the local community and its runaway world fame.

'There is always a fine line to be trodden between upholding our traditions and making sure that we continue to grow commercially,' says Ricken. Modern BVB still see themselves very much as a club of the Ruhr, and their website proudly boasts of 'deep roots in the culture of Dortmund and the surrounding region'. Yet they are also a global brand. According to Deloitte's Money League, they were the twelfth richest club in the world in 2023. Their international popularity has soared since the Jürgen Klopp era: they have thirteen official fan clubs in the UK alone, and countless others in countries as far flung as Iraq, Japan, Mexico and Sierra Leone. That is good for both the club and the city, but it also leaves Dortmund pulled in two directions.

Few embody that dilemma quite like Ricken. He is a born and bred local boy, an archetypal down-to-earth Dortmunder who is much loved among the club's traditional base. Though one of the most important figures at the club, his office is on the ground floor and he looks faintly amused when I address him with the polite *Sie* rather than the informal *Du*. As a player, he delivered one of the greatest moments in the club's history when he was just twenty-one, scoring a thirty-yard lob to win the 1997 Champions League final against Juventus. Marcel Reif's commentary ('Ricken... now lob him! *Jaaaa!*') immediately went down in Dortmund folklore and German television history, yet Ricken always remained rooted. 'Everyone around here still just knows me as Lars,' he told the club website in 2022.

Yet for all the salt-of-the-earth romanticism, Ricken is also very much part of brand BVB. Alongside others of the 1990s golden generation, he has long been one of the club's key brand ambassadors in emerging markets. 'When you go to Asia and you see people wearing black and yellow, that's a good feeling,' he says. 'As a Dortmunder by birth, I can say that we're not the most beautiful city in the world, but anyone who knows football knows Dortmund. And that makes me very proud.'

As academy director, he plays a key role in Dortmund's tightrope act between groundedness and growth. In recent years, BVB have developed a reputation as the elite finishing school of European football. Rather than attempting to outspend their richer rivals in England, Spain or Munich, they instead sign the most promising talents from across the world, give them time and space to develop, and sell them on at a significant profit. While some go straight into the Dortmund first team, others are signed at a younger age and make the step up to professionalism via Ricken's youth system. Either way, the Dortmund model is immensely successful. In recent years, it has helped polish some of the world's biggest stars in Real Madrid's Jude Bellingham to Manchester City's Erling Haaland, and also launched the careers of England's Jadon Sancho, France's Ousmane Dembélé and US internationals Christian Pulisic and Gio Reyna. It is an approach that has allowed BVB to grow and keep up with the European elite, while also maintaining a sustainable economic model, in line with the club's more humble roots.

Yet there are also downsides. By definition, Dortmund's model makes long-term squad-building more tricky, with the best players often sold on within one or two years of arriving. In order to attract the best young talent, meanwhile, it is far more important for Dortmund to be delivering reliable and regular Champions League football than it is for them to actually win trophies. Cynics argue that the club has lost its winning mentality, and while many at Dortmund roll their eyes at the accusation, there is no smoke without fire.

For a decade after the height of the Klopp era in 2012, Dortmund have been the undisputed second power in German football behind Bayern. But since Klopp, they have also launched only two serious title bids – in 2019 and 2023 – and fluffed both of them. After their Champions League Final appearance in 2013, they didn't reach the semi-finals for another eleven years. Between 2015 and 2023, they won just two of seventeen league games against Bayern. While Bayern's financial power certainly gives them a huge advantage, there is also a sense that Dortmund are a club in successful stagnation. As long as they keep finishing second or third, they will continue to attract the Bellinghams and Haalands. And as long as they do that, they in turn maintain their advantage over the rest of the league.

But is that really what football in the Ruhr is about? The steady management of second place? Ricken remembers standing on the terraces and watching grown men shake when Dortmund narrowly avoided relegation against Fortuna Köln in 1986. He remembers weeping when he scored a title-winning goal in 1995 to crown Dortmund champions for the first time in thirty-eight years. The emotional extremes, he says, are what make BVB so special. Yet aside from the harrowing shock of 2023, those extremes have been less of a feature in the club's more recent history.

Even on the fearsome Yellow Wall, things have sometimes felt a little flat. In both 2019 and 2023, the Dortmund ultras openly called for an improvement in the atmosphere, which they argued was not always living up to either its reputation or its own expectations. As Dortmund's talent factory becomes more and more of a production line, meanwhile, there are also fears that fans feel more and more detached from the stars on the pitch. In previous generations, the big stars coming out of BVB's youth system were players like Ricken, Marco Reus or Nuri Şahin, who had grown up in the local area and went on to spend much of their career at the club. The likes of Bellingham and Haaland, by contrast, are in and out before they even hit twenty-one.

Part of the academy's task, explains Ricken, is to maintain the bond between players and fans. As well as managing their sporting and personal development, he says, young BVB players are also taught to understand the club and its community, so as not to be completely divorced from the roots. He insists that many players are far more receptive to this than they are given credit for. US star Pulisic spoke perfect German within a year of arriving, he notes, while much-hyped teenage German striker Youssoufa Moukoko has stood alongside fans on the Yellow Wall. 'It's important that they get an idea of the fans who come to watch them as people, not just as this big yellow mass,' says Ricken.

The stadium, after all, remains the yardstick. Beyond the sepia tint of post-industrial nostalgia, it is on the terraces that the emotions and the traditions of football in the Ruhr still have some real-world meaning. In both the decline of Gelsenkirchen and the shine of Dortmund, the stadium is where the Ruhr's communities still come together to articulate some sense of self and find some link between the past and the present. If the atmosphere and the emotions are alive in the stadium, it is also a sign that the clubs themselves are walking the line between their industrial working-class roots and their modern commercial realities.

Ricken, who knows the Westfalenstadion as well as anyone, thinks that is still the case. 'I think we do pretty well,' he says. 'When you look at the atmosphere in the stadium, you can see it's not just people who are here because Borussia Dortmund are fashionable or are only here because of success. They are people who identify completely with this club. A lot has changed in this city and this region, but the pride in their football club? People still have that.'

But it remains a constant balancing act – and not just in the Ruhr. In other regions too, clubs and communities are grappling with similar questions about how to maintain international success without losing touch with your roots. And there is one industry in particular where that has always been a million-dollar question. The Ruhr may always have been the engine of German industry. But it was Stuttgart, way down in the south-west, that produced its most famous motor.

STUTTGART (SWABIA)

4

STUTTGART
MADE IN SWABIA

Gottlieb Daimler was already in his early fifties when he became Stuttgart's most famous son. His neatly trimmed beard had already begun to turn white, while the rest of his head had long since surrendered to baldness. He had three sons, two daughters and a thick-coated retriever named Bello. Having travelled across Germany and Europe as a young man, he had now settled in his native Stuttgart, started his own company, and built himself a grand home near one of the city's natural springs. It was there, pottering around in what was effectively a glorified garden shed, that he perfected the device that would change human history forever.

Daimler had always been a machine man. He trained as a gunsmith in his teenage years, and later waltzed through his studies in Stuttgart and Alsace to become a qualified engineer by his mid-twenties. In the early 1860s, he spent two years in England, seeing the seismic effects of the Industrial Revolution up close in the machinery and locomotive factories of Manchester, Leeds, Oldham and Coventry.

Yet if Britain had long been the motor of change in Europe, Germany was by now also beginning to clunk into gear. By the

1870s, the mining industries in the Ruhr were in full swing and German industry was beginning to produce its own commercial powerhouses and innovations. In 1872, Daimler and his protégé Wilhelm Maybach started working for Nicolaus Otto, a Cologne-based inventor who had already created one of the first internal combustion engines. Otto, whose Deutz company would later become one of the continent's major engine manufacturers, never quite saw eye to eye with Daimler. The two men clashed bitterly over patents and the company's direction, and they parted ways in a blaze of acrimony in 1880.

Daimler moved back to Stuttgart, taking Maybach with him and setting up anew in the old Roman spa town of Bad Cannstatt. Never one for dreaming small, he built himself a villa just across the river from the old Roman fort, complete with an outdoor gallery, a small garden workshop, and a tower to which he could retreat in moments of introspection. In the years that followed, he and Maybach continued to work on the engines they had begun developing at Deutz and were in and out of the patent office for much of the early 1880s. The biggest breakthrough came in 1885, with a tall vertical-cylinder motor they nicknamed 'the grandfather clock'.

The 'grandfather clock' was revolutionary in two ways. The first was that it ran on petroleum, rather than the gas engines favoured by Otto. The second was that it was mobile, meaning it could be attached to vehicles of all kinds. A few months after submitting the patent application, Daimler fitted it to a two-wheeled 'riding wagon', which his youngest son Adolf duly took for a test drive through Bad Cannstatt, reaching mind-boggling speeds of twelve kilometres per hour. The world's first motorcycle – and indeed its first biker – had been born.

Daimler's ultimate vision – later immortalised in his company's famous three-spired logo – was to conquer the air, the land and the sea. Within a few years, he had attached his motor to all kinds of vehicles, including a railcar, a boat and even an airship. In most cases, he would demonstrate their reliability himself, proudly motoring across a local lake in his bowler hat and cane or rumbling down to the Wasn festival grounds in a motorised railcar. Yet there was one invention in particular that really changed the world. In 1886, he fixed his engine to a four-seater 'Americaine' horse carriage, creating the first ever four-wheeled automobile.

Whether or not Daimler counts as the inventor of the car is up for debate. In truth, he was probably beaten to the punch by Carl Benz, a fellow south-westerner who had developed a similar three-wheeled vehicle up the road in Mannheim around the same time. Yet Daimler had played his role, and when his and Benz's companies merged in the 1920s, they created what is still one of the most instantly recognisable automobile brands in the world. Alongside others like Volkswagen, BMW and Stuttgart neighbours Porsche, it has become one of several German companies that have dominated the sector for almost a century. For years, the firm was known as 'Daimler-Benz'. As of 2022, its official name is the 'Mercedes-Benz Group', in honour of its most famous product.

One thing, though, has not changed since Daimler and Maybach officially founded it as Daimler Motoren Gesellschaft in 1890. Now as then, the company's headquarters are still on the Bad Cannstatt side of Stuttgart's Neckar river, just a stone's throw from Daimler's former home. The villa itself was destroyed in the Second World War, but the gallery, the tower and the garden workshop are still there, on the edge of a public park just two

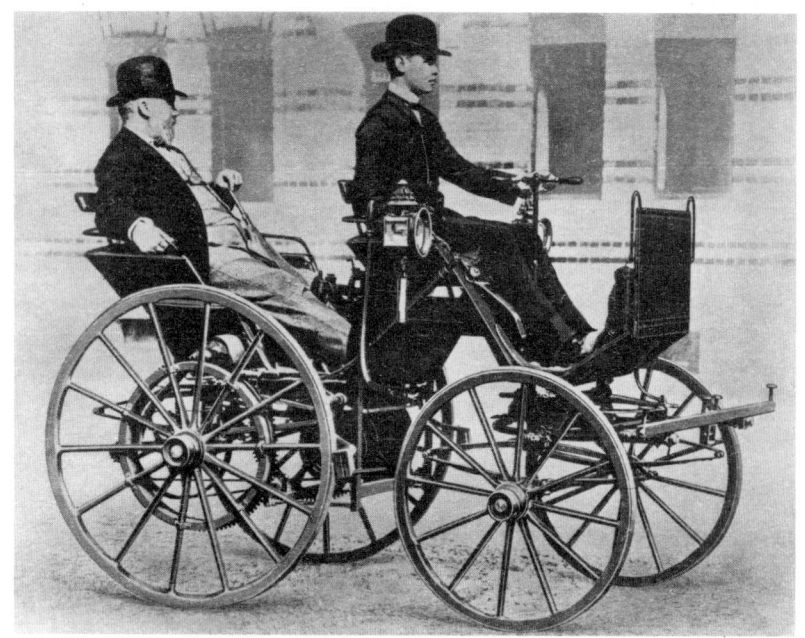

Gottlieb Daimler rides in his 1886 'motor-carriage', one of the world's first automobiles. © Mercedes-Benz Classic

or three tram stops up the hill from Bad Cannstatt station. The workshop, not much bigger than a greenhouse, contains a small free-to-visit exhibition on Daimler's inventions.

Stuttgart remains intensely proud of Daimler, and with good reason. Mercedes-Benz is still the city's biggest employer, with around 41,000 residents working for the company in 2019. Even for a company with outposts in forty-three countries, the sprawling hometown plant in Stuttgart-Untertürkheim is still a significant part of the global production line. On its western edge, just inside Bad Cannstatt, the Mercedes-Benz Museum attracts more than half a million tourists a year. And perhaps most importantly, the company's location puts it right at the heart of Stuttgart's soul. As you approach the Mercedes complex from the city centre, you pass two locations that are part of the city's cultural lifeblood. On the right, there is the Cannstatter Wasen, which hosts huge fairs and beer festivals in spring and autumn. On the left, there is the football stadium.

VfB Stuttgart are arguably the city's third most famous export after Mercedes and Porsche. As five-time champions, three-time cup winners and three-time European finalists, they are one of the most successful clubs in Germany and, until Leverkusen's triumph in 2024, one of the last to win the Bundesliga title other than Bayern and Dortmund. They are one of several clubs in Germany who have traditionally stood not just for their district or their city, but also for the entire surrounding region, with a fanbase that stretches across the country and almost no other club of their stature for 200 kilometres in any direction. Instantly recognisable by their white shirts with the red stripe across the chest, they are one of the clubs that can consider themselves German football royalty. And for a long time at least, that was also down to Mercedes-Benz.

VfB have long had a special relationship with the city's most famous car manufacturer. The football club was also founded in Bad Cannstatt, and its 60,000-seater stadium sits right on the edge of the Mercedes complex. For decades, the company was VfB's biggest and most loyal sponsor, putting their products on the front of the shirts, supporting the club's social projects and maintaining an almost constant presence on the club board. Along with Volkswagen at VfL Wolfsburg and Audi at Bayern Munich, they are one of several major German car companies that are at least partial owners of a Bundesliga club.

Football and the automobile industry are often natural bedfellows, but nowhere are they more intimately entwined than in Germany. For Germans the car is more than just a product or a status symbol. It is a national icon. Ever since it was invented by

Daimler and Benz, the automobile has been an indelible part of the German story. Having emerged from Germany's rapid rise as an industrial power in the nineteenth century, it was cleverly instrumentalised by the Nazi propaganda and war machines, before becoming a symbol of the country's economic and political recovery in both East and West after the Second World War. For half a century until the mid-2000s, the Federal Republic ranked consistently among the top three car-producing countries in the world. It still manufactures more cars than any other European nation, while the car industry as a whole employs almost a million people across the country. The sector is also a lynchpin of Germany's export-heavy economy, making up around seventeen per cent of all overseas sales in 2023.[5] The car, in other words, is the very essence of 'Made in Germany'.

Germans, in turn, are obsessive motorists. One in four Germans are members of the country's automobile association, ADAC, which is by far the largest in Europe. As of 2024, Germany is still the only country in the world with no official speed limit on its motorways, a status quo that is furiously defended by certain political parties as a point of principle. For millions of people across the country, cars are more than vehicles. They are a part of many people's personal and professional identity. For that reason, the car companies' involvement in football is about more than just boosting sales. It is a way of reinforcing their status as a part of the nation's identity. It is a way of ensuring that, even as world-famous global brands, they never lose touch with their roots.

In the case of Mercedes, and their equally famous neighbours Porsche, those roots are in Stuttgart and the south-west. They are in VfB country, among the people who hail from the former kingdom of Württemberg, and are known culturally and linguistically as *Schwaben*, or Swabians. To the rest of the world, the luxury cars of Mercedes and Porsche are Made in Germany. To Germans, they are Made in Swabia.

Stuttgart is one of the few corners of Germany where beer is not king. The city has its fair share of old taverns which, on the face of it, are much the same as all German pubs. They have the same wood-panelled interiors, the same medieval lack of natural light, and the same dusty photo frames hanging on the walls. The tables host the same groups of elderly men playing skat, grumbling about the football and wondering whether they can stretch their wallets and watches to one more drink. The landlords and landladies, meanwhile, rule their domain with the same dictatorial benevolence. There is no scrum at the bar: as a drinker, your tab is notched up with a biro on the edge of your beer mat, to be paid at the end with the obligatory ten per cent tip. The only difference is that in Stuttgart, the pub is more likely to call itself a *Weinstube*, and the drink of choice is more likely to be a Riesling, a Silvaner or a Spätburgunder. This is wine country, a region of slopes and valleys which lies just far south enough to support grape vines.

It was, supposedly, the Romans who first brought viticulture to the region. The Germanic tribes may have beaten them back further north, but in the west and south-west, the Romans left their mark in Germany as much as anywhere else in Western Europe. They laid the foundations for what is now Stuttgart in the first century AD, building a fort at the natural springs of Bad

Cannstatt as an outpost between the larger centres like Cologne, Trier, Mainz and Augsburg. Stuttgart itself only emerged as a major settlement centuries later in the medieval period, and there is little trace of the Romans there now. But the wine has stayed, and Bad Cannstatt is still proud of its ancient roots.

It may officially have been a borough of Stuttgart for more than a hundred years, but many are still quick to make the distinction between this district and the rest of the city. While the centre of Stuttgart is marked by huge eighteenth-century squares and wide modern shopping streets, Bad Cannstatt is more Gothic. The old town is a cobbled warren of claustrophobic half-timbered buildings, including a fourteenth-century monastery-turned-pub which is the oldest standing house in the city. The VfB Stuttgart ultras refer to themselves as 'Commando Cannstatt', while fans of Stuttgarter Kickers, the city's smaller and older club, will tell you that they are the real Stuttgart team. 'Stuttgart ends on the banks of the Neckar,' they joke.

In reality, though, the Kickers have long resigned themselves to the role of second fiddle. Their stadium, which is six times smaller than VfB's, sits at the foot of the Stuttgart television tower on a hill overlooking the city from the south-east. From the top of the tower, you can see not only the sweep of the city, right out to Bad Cannstatt and the Mercedes-Benz plant up in the north, but also the wine slopes and luscious green forests which stretch out beyond the town itself. It is a region known colloquially as Swabia. And aside from the little blue stadium at the foot of the tower, Swabia is VfB country.

Where Swabia begins and ends is hard to say. Officially speaking, Stuttgart is the capital of the federal state of Baden-Württemberg, which, as its name suggests, is made up of two historical kingdoms. Baden slopes up the French border and includes cities like Freiburg, Heidelberg and Karlsruhe as well as most of the Black Forest. The eastern half is Württemberg, which contains Stuttgart, Heilbronn and Ulm. Culturally speaking, they are two very different regions and it is in Württemberg where people would consider themselves *Schwaben*, or Swabians. Yet as with so many German regions, Swabia is an idea that exists more in people's heads than on a map.

'Being Swabian for me is about being embedded in the culture,' says Guido Buchwald. A legendary midfielder and World Cup winner with Germany in 1990, Buchwald is as Swabian as they come. He was born in West Berlin, but moved to Stuttgart as a baby and has been there almost non-stop ever since. He spent most of his playing career at Kickers and VfB, and as he explains, he and almost all of his extended family still live within a stone's throw of the city. 'That's the nice thing about football. You can travel the world and meet people from all over, but without losing touch with your roots,' he says.

So what does it mean to have Swabian roots? On the one hand, it is a linguistic thing. *Schwäbisch* is a very different kind of German to the one spoken in Baden or Bavaria, a cutesy dialect, in which almost everything is given the *suffix –le*. A glass of wine in a pub is known as a *Viertele* or an *Achtele* depending on the size, and the iconic, winding stone steps which are dotted around the cityscape in Stuttgart are known as *Stäffele*. The region itself is often simply called the *Ländle* or 'little country'. It is also known for its culinary flare: Stuttgart itself is considered a gastro-capital, and Swabia has some of the most widely loved traditional dishes in the country. As well as the obligatory pork roasts, they also include ravioli-like *Maultaschen* and handmade *Käsespätzle*, an iron pan of noodles fried in copious amounts of cheese and sprinkled with chives for the illusion of decency.

Swabians also have a certain reputation in the rest of the country. 'We are known for being solid, hard-working and careful with money. Depending on who you ask, that can be a good or a bad thing,' says Buchwald. Germany is a society still haunted by the hyperinflation of the 1920s, when the value of the national currency plummeted to billions of marks to the dollar and people pushed wheelbarrows of banknotes through the streets. Nowadays, the country is notoriously allergic to the idea of debt and overspending. Restrictions on government debt are baked in to the constitution, and until the Covid pandemic, governments kept religiously to the golden rule of the 'black zero', which dictated that the state's outgoings should never exceed its income. The Germans themselves also often rank among the most diligent savers in Europe. They pay huge down payments on properties to avoid large mortgages, and grumble furiously whenever the European Central Bank lowers interest rates. Yet in a nation of piggy-bank owners, it is the Swabians who stand out. Politicians and journalists often talk about the 'Swabian housewife' as an archetype of German thriftiness.

Like most stereotypes, it tends to get mixed up with others. While Bavaria and Baden are popular holiday destinations, known for their hospitality and joie de vivre, Swabia can often seem a bit more dour. As one cruel joke has it: 'When they need to laugh, Swabians go down into the cellar.' Buchwald, though, insists this is a misconception. The Stuttgart legend spent a few years in Japan playing for the Urawa Red Diamonds in the mid-1990s, and he compares the Swabians to the Japanese. 'They are known for being very polite and meticulous, but if you go a bit deeper and really get to know them, you see that they also really enjoy life,' he says. 'In Baden, people are a bit more easy-going, they open up a bit more quickly. In Swabia, it takes longer to make friends with people, but when you do, you have a very intense friendship that will probably last a lifetime.'

Perhaps only a Stuttgarter could go all the way to Japan and conclude that, ultimately, the land of the rising sun was just Swabia by another name. Yet in some ways, Buchwald's own biography proves his point. He talks about Japan as a home away from home, and is still considered a legend in Urawa, having made a huge impact in his two spells there as a player and a manager. While other players of his era followed the money to Munich, Italy and elsewhere, Buchwald had one meaningful love affair with Japan and otherwise remained firmly rooted in the south-west. As a player, he came up through the ranks at Stuttgarter Kickers before spending a decade at VfB. He has remained loyal to both clubs since he retired in 1999, serving as a board member at VfB and a director of sport and interim head coach at the Kickers. 'Both Stuttgart clubs are very close to my heart,' he says.

That is not entirely unusual. The gulf in quality between VfB and the Kickers is such that there isn't much of a genuine rivalry between the two clubs. Sponsors are often involved with both of them at the same time, and Buchwald is far from the only player to have graduated from the Kickers' youth system into first-division success at VfB. Former US national team coach Jürgen Klinsmann also followed the same path in the early 1980s, joining the bigger club just a year after Buchwald in 1984.

Klinsmann's father ran a bakery on the outskirts of Stuttgart, and even in English his accent still sounds unmistakably Swabian. Yet the prolific goal scorer with flowing blond hair was arguably always too much of a showman to stay in the Ländle. He left VfB in 1989 to pursue a career which took him to Inter Milan, Bayern, Monaco and Tottenham Hotspur. His goals – and some would say his theatrics – helped West Germany win a third World Cup in the summer of 1990, and as a manager, he helped reinvent the national team's image at the home World Cup in 2006 before going on to have success with the USA. Yet Klinsmann's smooth-talking charm – his very Americanness – was always divisive. In 2009, just after an ill-fated spell in charge of Bayern Munich, German chat show host Günther Jauch referred to him as 'the Obama of German football'. A few months later, Bayern president Uli Hoeness shot back: 'If he's Obama, then I'm Mother Teresa'.

Buchwald, by contrast, was always more typically Swabian. As a conversationalist, he is friendly and polite, but no more than that. As a player, he was the opposite of Klinsmann: an industrious defensive midfielder known for his thunderous long-range shots and ferocious slide tackles. During the 1990 World Cup, his teammates were so surprised to see he had any close ball control in training that they nicknamed him 'Diego' in reference to the great Argentinian Maradona. In the final, he marked the real Diego out of the game.

Unsurprisingly, those qualities also made him a legend at VfB Stuttgart, where he was part of one of the most successful teams in the club's history. 'VfB were a much bigger name back then than they are now, because we were always up near the top of the league,' he explains. Buchwald won the title in his first season at Stuttgart, and in the course of the 1980s, VfB quickly established themselves as the country's third power alongside Bayern and Hamburg. 'In the eleven seasons I was there, we qualified for Europe ten times. If we finished seventh, it would be a major crisis,' he says.

Buchwald was captain by the time he won his second title with Stuttgart, clinching the trophy with a late header in one of the most dramatic season finales the Bundesliga has ever seen. VfB, Borussia Dortmund and Eintracht Frankfurt had all gone into the final day tied on fifty points. While Frankfurt slumped to a shock defeat away to Hansa Rostock, Buchwald scored an eighty-eighth-minute header in Leverkusen to send Stuttgart top. At that point, he says, there was genuine hope that the club could become a major European power to rival Bayern. But it didn't turn out that way. Stuttgart may have won the title in 2007, making them one of the few clubs aside from Bayern and Dortmund to have done so in the twenty-first century, but aside from that one high point, they have struggled to live up to their once grand name. In the 2010s, they suffered relegation from the Bundesliga twice in the space of five years, joining the likes of Köln, Hamburg, Schalke and Gladbach on the long list of German football's fallen giants.

The stagnation and decline of the big Traditionsvereine has been a running theme in recent decades. In theory, these are clubs that have all the ingredients to emulate the success of Bayern and, more recently, Dortmund. They have a huge fanbase across the region, a long tradition of on-field success, and, in Stuttgart's case, an enormously wealthy global corporation on their doorstep. Yet instead of flourishing, they have floundered, and often for very similar reasons.

On the one hand, they have a tendency to tear themselves apart. Having a whole region behind you is good from one perspective, but it also means that everybody wants a piece of the action. In the modern era, clubs of Stuttgart's size have often struggled to marry the competing demands of fans, sponsors, politicians and other stakeholders. 'Everyone always thinks they know best. When you have a lot of fans and a lot people, you are going to get different factions,' says Buchwald. That often leaves the club in turmoil, pulled this way and that between competing visions. Stuttgart's return to the Bundesliga in 2020, for example, was overshadowed by reports that the club had illegally passed on members' personal data to third parties, a scandal which unleashed a bitter power struggle between president Claus Vogt and chairman Thomas Hitzlsperger. At its height, Hitzlsperger accused Vogt of 'threatening the club's continued existence' and announced a bid to run against him as president in early 2021. He later pulled out of the race, but the dispute still divided the fanbase and left a sour taste for years afterwards.

Buchwald is no stranger to such infighting. He himself resigned as a board member in 2019 in the midst of a squabble over the VfB's sporting direction. Even a few years on, he still has strong views about who is to blame for Stuttgart's recent decline. He names a few former sporting directors who were hired on the basis of their success elsewhere but failed to emulate that success at VfB. 'The club was put into the hands of people who weren't from the region and didn't understand the club's DNA, and they tried to change everything,' he says.

This is also a recurring theme in German football. In recent years, smaller clubs with deeper roots in their local communities have had more success than the traditional giants who have fans across the entire country. That is particularly apparent in the south-west, where Stuttgart have struggled and clubs like Mainz, Freiburg and Heidenheim have begun to punch far above their weight. Even Hoffenheim are, to some extent, an example of a local club done good. Though widely seen as one of the Bundesliga's plastic nouveaux-riches, they are at least bankrolled primarily by local billionaire Dietmar Hopp and his software company SAP.

There are other reasons for the increasing success of smaller clubs, not least the benefit of lower expectations. 'Obviously there is more pressure at a club like VfB, where you have 80,000 members and so much history, and that does make it more difficult,' says Buchwald. He insists that the club should still be aiming to establish itself long-term as 'one of the top six or seven' in Germany but admits that a sustained return to the glory years won't happen overnight. 'It will take time to regain the aura that VfB used to have in this country, and you have to work up from the bottom,' he says.

Yet he is also adamant that size can be an advantage. 'VfB is a sleeping giant, or a big locomotive. It takes time to get it rolling, but once it gets going, it has so much power,' he says. Stuttgart, after all, still have everything going for them. They are still by far the biggest club in Swabia, and arguably the biggest in the whole of the south-west. Perhaps most importantly of all, they are a club from Bad Cannstatt, who are quite literally cut from the same cloth as a company like Mercedes-Benz.

That hasn't prevented them from imploding before. But as of 2023, Stuttgart don't just have Mercedes driving them forward. They also have Porsche. And especially in a country like Germany, that is a hell of a lot of horsepower.

Lutz Meschke has a big smile on his face. A few months previously, VfB Stuttgart were in the doldrums. They had just narrowly avoided relegation for the second year in a row and were gearing up for another depressingly mediocre Bundesliga season. But then

Porsche pulled up, and suddenly everything seemed to change. It is now October 2023, and the club are enjoying their best start to a season in years. 'It's nice to have some success: we are all very happy,' says Meschke, Porsche's deputy chairman and CFO.

The fifty-seven-year-old is exactly what you might expect from a director at a major sports car manufacturer. His silvery black hair is slicked back like Gordon Gekko's, and he smiles with his eyes in a way that tells you to just sit back and enjoy the ride. He has been at Porsche for over twenty years and has had a seat on the executive board as CFO since 2009. In 2022, German financial newspaper *Handelsblatt* described him as 'Porsche's secret midfield playmaker'.

On the other hand, Meschke also knows enough about football to not get carried away with VfB's good run of form. He grew up near Mönchengladbach, played for his local club, and spent his youth watching Borussia from the terraces of the Bökelberg. Nowadays, he is a regular guest in the VIP boxes at Stuttgart, and has a habit of getting his company involved with football projects. For years, Porsche has supported youth development initiatives at Gladbach, Leipzig and both Stuttgart clubs. When the chance came to take on a bigger role at VfB in the summer of 2023, Meschke jumped at it. 'This club is so big in the region. It's the club that most of the people who work for us support. We couldn't not get involved,' he says.

Even so, the deal that Porsche and VfB announced in June 2023 made significant waves in Stuttgart. The city's two major car companies tend to avoid treading on each other's toes, and the football club had traditionally been Mercedes territory. VfB's stadium, after all, lies just over the road from the Mercedes-Benz HQ, within walking distance of Gottlieb Daimler's former villa in Bad Cannstatt. It was known as the Mercedes-Benz Arena from 2008 to 2023, and as the Gottlieb-Daimler-Stadion before that. Porsche's headquarters, by contrast, lie a little further out in the district of Zuffenhausen, and their involvement with VfB had traditionally been limited.

By the early 2020s, though, rumours had been circling for some time that Mercedes were planning to scale down their involvement with VfB. After a decade of almost constant crises on and off the field, the car company's love affair with the club was under strain. In 2023, both parties decided to shake things up by bringing Porsche on board in a deal which VfB sporting director Alexander Wehrle claimed was worth around 100 million euros. While Mercedes would remain one of Stuttgart's 'anchor investors', Porsche now also began to acquire shares in the club. The stadium on Mercedes's doorstep, meanwhile, was renamed after the IT and management consultancy MHP, a Porsche subsidiary.

Meschke admits it is unusual for the two car companies to rub up so close to each other. Yet he says they have a good relationship and insists that Porsche's deal with Stuttgart is not about stealing a march on their rivals. 'Replacing Mercedes wouldn't have brought the club much further at all. We want to help create a spirit of change, and we can only do that alongside Mercedes and other businesses in the region. If you don't work together, then you have no chance of being competitive,' he says.

Like Buchwald, he is keenly aware of how petty factionalism and disunity have hamstrung Stuttgart in recent years. 'We want to play an active role in the way the club is run,' he says, but insists that is more about channelling Porsche's business expertise than about making the club into a kind of Porsche FC. 'These clubs are businesses with high revenues and a lot of employees, but often they are not run as professionally as they should be,' he says. 'People use them as a platform to profile themselves and make themselves feel important. But in reality, it's not about any individual person or any individual sponsor, but about the club. You need everyone pulling in the same direction.'

But if the club is such a mess, why get involved at all? In the end, it is simply good for Porsche's brand identity to be involved with a club like VfB. Not so much because they are successful, but because they embody a kind of regional pride which is also integral to the self-image of companies like Porsche and Mercedes. At the press conference at which the new partnership was unveiled, Meschke talked about 'pooling resources: from the region, for the region', and he insists that is more than just lip service. Porsche's logo contains both the rearing black horse from Stuttgart's coat of arms, and the three antlers of Württemberg which are also in VfB's badge.

'Our roots are here in Swabia,' says Meschke, though he admits that the Swabian traits of humility and thriftiness aren't always perfect values for a luxury sports car manufacturer. On the other hand, that is also the very nature of the German export model. The Swabians don't need to buy Porsches, they just need to make them. And in that regard, their hard-working, no-frills style is the biggest strength a company like Porsche has. For people across the world, the phrase 'Made in Germany' is a byword for reliability and high-quality engineering. But as Meschke points out, that only holds up if the products are, in fact, made in Germany. 'We develop in Germany and we produce in Germany: that is a very important basis for us as an international luxury brand. It's a bit like with Swiss watches: in order to be a luxury good, they do have to be made in Switzerland,' he says. In truth, Porsche produces its Cayenne model in Bratislava and previously had a production line in Finland. But it is true that the vast majority of their cars are still produced in Stuttgart-Zuffenhausen and Leipzig.

There is, however, more to 'Made in Germany' than the big poster boys like Porsche and Mercedes. Ask most experts, and they will say that the backbone of the German economy, as well as its reputation for high-quality exports, is the so-called *Mittelstand*. These are the small and medium-sized, often family-run enterprises which make up more than ninety-nine per cent of the country's registered businesses. In the car industry as in others, it is these smaller companies that supposedly breathe life into the German manufacturing machine, whether as service providers and suppliers, as producers, or as training grounds for talent.

That is obviously not just a German thing. The European Commission estimates that small and medium-sized enterprises account for more than half of EU gross domestic product. Yet nowhere do they enjoy such hallowed cultural status as in Germany. As the word itself suggests, the Mittelstand is more than just economic jargon. It is an expression of a deep-rooted business culture, a kind of self-mythology among the German middle class. To be of the Mittelstand is to be of the very bulk of German society. The idea of the small, family-run business which quietly delivers high quality and doesn't cut corners is, for many, the ultimate paragon of Germanness.

Even for a world-famous brand like Porsche, paying homage to that myth remains hugely important. 'We are a global brand, but we still feel like a medium-sized family business. For me, that means that people feel like it is also their company, or even their

The Porsche logo features the antlers of Württemberg, which are also part of VfB Stuttgart's badge. © 2023 Dr. Ing. h.c. F. Porsche AG

family. They aren't just employees, they actually identify with Porsche. They almost feel like they own it, and that means they go the extra mile,' says Meschke. Along with Bosch, Aldi and others, Porsche is one of many internationally successful German companies that are still partially owned and run by the family that founded them. 'Wolfgang Porsche, the founder's grandson, is still chairman of the supervisory board, and the family still plays a very active role. That sense of family is very important to us,' says Meschke.

So it makes sense when Meschke says that sponsoring VfB Stuttgart is more about Porsche's corporate social responsibility than it is about reaching potential consumers. He points out that the Stuttgarter Kickers are also part of Porsche's *Turbo für Talente* initiative, which helps young athletes make their first steps in professional sport. In a country where family comes first, regional roots matter and the Mittelstand is king, it is simply good PR to help the local football club. And in recent years, good PR has been in short supply for the German car industry.

The automobile sector may still be a huge part of the German economy, but the days in which it was a universally trusted and uncontroversial part of German society are now long gone. In 2015, it emerged that Porsche's parent company Volkswagen had been deliberately cheating on emissions tests to make their diesel-fuelled cars appear significantly more environmentally friendly than they were in reality. The scandal, in which many other German and European car manufacturers were also implicated, was an unprecedented body blow for the industry. For Volkswagen alone, it ended in billions of dollars of fines, countless consumer lawsuits, and even criminal indictments against certain directors, including former Bayern Munich board member Martin Winterkorn.

Since then, the sector has had to work hard to regain trust, especially against the backdrop of an ever more fierce public debate about climate change and environmental protection. At the same time, the global standing of Germany's car producers has also begun to look more shaky. On the international stage, German companies are facing increasingly tough competition from their rivals in China and the US. Chinese electric vehicle producers are increasing their market share in Europe, while Elon Musk's Tesla opened its first European gigafactory in Berlin in 2021.

Meschke is one of those sounding the alarm bells. 'The situation is not an easy one right now. In certain areas like electrification, battery technology and digitalisation, European car manufacturers have already fallen behind the market leaders. That is just a fact. We have a lot of catching up to do,' he says, adding that many underestimate how precarious the situation is. 'At the moment, the overall results are still good, but they are based on old technologies. If we don't invest in the technologies of the future in Europe, the continent will lose jobs, and that will be a huge problem for our prosperity.'

He would say that, of course. The German automobile industry is well versed in the art of defending its own interests. It has the fifth-largest lobbying organisation on the German parliamentary register, spending more than nine million euros a year on political lobbying alone.[6] That clout also extends to Europe, and in 2023, the German government unleashed a weeks-long stand-off in Brussels when it withdrew support for an EU draft law banning new combustion engines from 2035. Meschke himself is also a diligent lobbyist for his sector, often writing editorials calling for deregulation in the European market. He has repeatedly made the case that it is not just the future of the car industry at stake, but that of liberal democracy per se. 'Our prosperity is built on freedom, and our freedom is built on prosperity,' he says. 'If we don't have that prosperity anymore, it is going to become very difficult for us to maintain that basis of democracy. And that is something we need to defend with everything we have.'

It is strong language. The kind that is typical of an increasingly emotional German conversation about cars and the car industry. Politics in Germany has often been less polarised than in the US or the UK, yet cars are one of a few issues where there are two increasingly entrenched sides of an intractable culture war. The coalition government which took office in 2021 remained bitterly divided over the issue of the speed limit, as well as over e-fuels and the future of the combustion engine. Meschke claims the car is 'a symbol of individual freedom'. Critics of the car industry counter that Germany is as religious about its cars as the US is about its guns.

Whatever one thinks of Meschke's arguments about democracy, the fact that he is even making it says a lot about how much the automobile matters in Germany. The success of the car industry was a fundamental cornerstone of Germany's post-war economic miracle, its rehabilitation as a prosperous, democratic country. Even now, that still gives the car an immense symbolic power.

Meschke, meanwhile, is far from the only person who is concerned for the future of democracy. Just two weeks before our interview, the newly appointed chairman of the German Football League, Marc Lenz, told the *Frankfurter Rundschau* newspaper that he too was concerned about the political situation in Germany. 'It will be football's task to use its societal reach to defend democracy and democratic values,' he said. A few months later in early 2024, Freiburg coach Christian Streich led a wave of calls for football to stand up and be counted in the fight against far-right extremism. 'I am very grateful to have lived as a free person in a democracy for fifty-eight years,' he said. 'Anyone who doesn't stand up now has not understood the lessons of history.'

Whether in parliament, in business or in football, the idea that democracy might suddenly fail is ever present in Germany. To understand why, you have to travel an hour north from Stuttgart on the train, to the city in which German democracy was born.

FRANKFURT (HESSE)

5

FRANKFURT
NATION BUILDING

Franz Beckenbauer stood wide-eyed in the grand *Kaisersaal* of Frankfurt's city hall, an emperor in the Hall of Emperors. Centuries ago, this room was where the German kings of the Holy Roman Empire were crowned. And now here he was, the man they had always called *der Kaiser*, waiting to go out onto the balcony in front of his adoring subjects. As the somewhat excitable TV reporter in front of him put it: 'They crowned Franz II in here once: now I think we'll crown you Franz III!'

Beckenbauer smiled his patient smile. The real coronation had come the night before in Rome, when his side had beaten Argentina 1–0 to claim a third World Cup title for West Germany. Sixteen years after captaining his team to the trophy on home soil in 1974, Beckenbauer was one of only two men to have become world champion as both a player and a manager. It was only fitting that he was now back in the Römer, the three-gabled medieval house in the heart of Frankfurt's old town. This was where the great German teams had always returned to after tournaments abroad, to parade in front of the fans on the intricately carved terracotta balcony that looked over the Römerberg square. Beckenbauer had first appeared here as a player in 1966, when West Germany had returned from England as losing World Cup finalists. He had come again in 1970 and 1986. And now he was back, this time with the trophy in hand.

It had taken twice as long to get from the airport this time, because the streets were packed with fans and the cavalcade had been stopped on every corner. The Kaisersaal itself was also fit to burst, the players having to squeeze through a crowd of photographers, reporters and DFB bigwigs. As they finally emerged onto the balcony, the sloping cobbled square below was completely awash with flags of black, red and gold. 'I've never seen anything like it. This is by far the biggest and the nicest reception we've ever had,' Beckenbauer told the TV reporter.

The 1990 World Cup win had come at a moment of intense national optimism, just nine months after the fall of the Berlin Wall and three months before official reunification. Yet even then – and even for an old national treasure like Beckenbauer – the sight of hundreds of Germans waving their national flag was still unusual. In Germany, the flag is a far less present feature of public life than, say, the Union Jack in Britain or the Stars and Stripes in the USA. The monarchy is long gone, meaning there are no coronations, jubilees or royal weddings. Even 3 October – the anniversary of reunification and the closest thing Germany has to a 4 July – rarely prompts wild displays of public patriotism. The only time the flag seems to wave from every window is during a major football tournament, and even then it tends to raise eyebrows.

The black, red and gold horizontal tricolour was first adopted as the national flag in 1848, the year in which revolution swept through Europe. In Germany, that led to the creation of a first ever

Black, red and gold was first used as the national flag in 1848, when Germany's first ever national parliament convened in the Paulskirche in Frankfurt. © Historisches Museum Frankfurt C12527

elected national parliament, which convened at the Paulskirche in Frankfurt, just across the road from the Römer city hall. The National Assembly of 1848 was the first to lay down a democratic constitution and articulate civil and human rights for German citizens. It also immortalised the black, red and gold as a symbol of democracy, revolution, and, above all, the sovereignty of the German people over any of the old regional monarchies.

Which was all well and good. Except the 1848 revolution ultimately failed. The Frankfurt parliament collapsed after barely a year, leaving Germany once again in the hands of the old kings and Kaisers. When the country was finally unified under Bismarck's Prussia in 1871, the newly established German Empire chose a different flag, one which combined the black and white of Prussia with the red of various other German states. These colours represented a different vision of Germany:

imperial, expansionist and militaristic. They were later adopted by the National Socialist Party of German Workers (NSDAP), which seized power and established a fascist dictatorship in 1933. And it was the crimes of that regime that changed the debate around German national identity forever.

In the twelve years of Nazi rule from 1933 to 1945, an estimated seventeen million people died as a result of German crimes against humanity. Approximately six million of those were Jewish victims of the Shoah, an unprecedented act of genocide in which the Germans and their collaborators systematically persecuted and murdered Europe's Jewish population on the basis of a racist ideology. In just over a decade, what began with the removal of rights, ghettoisation and forced expropriation morphed into a system of planned industrial mass murder. In total, around two-thirds of Europe's pre-war Jewish population were murdered in the Holocaust. Of those, around half died in extermination camps such as Auschwitz. Millions of others were executed in mass shootings, mobile gas vans and other acts of chilling inhumanity: all of it carried out in the name of the German nation.[7]

How do you go on after that? How do you express any kind of pride in a nation that has committed such heinous acts? As the occupying Allied powers rebuilt Germany after the Second World War, symbolism mattered. Just like the Weimar Republic before them, both post-war Germanies returned to the black, red and gold flag, picking up the democratic tradition of 1848. In American-occupied Frankfurt, the Paulskirche was one of the very first old town buildings to be rebuilt from the rubble. Nowadays, the building is a kind of shrine to democracy. Its outer walls bear plaques honouring figures like US President John F. Kennedy and West Germany's first democratic post-war

President, Theodor Heuss. Inside, there is a modern rendering of the 1848 parliament, with chairs arranged in a horseshoe around a central pulpit, and the flags of the modern federal states hanging from the whitewashed walls.

But it is one thing to rebuild churches and hoist new flags, and quite another to reconstruct society. The Nazis, after all, had used democratic means to destroy democracy, and the Holocaust had been carried out with at least the tacit acceptance of the German people. At the Großmarkthalle memorial site in Frankfurt, where tens of thousands of Jews from the city and the region of Hesse were deported to the camps and ghettos in the east, you can still read the harrowing testimonies of victims and eyewitnesses alike. In one of them, a non-Jewish woman remembers watching Gestapo officers guard trains crammed with people. 'I wasn't the only one who knew what was happening,' she wrote. 'Lots of people knew.'

Modern Germany is a country built on the knowledge of its past crimes. Its frank and self-critical approach to Nazi history has been a key part of its rehabilitation as a peaceful, democratic European nation. But that approach did not develop overnight. It was and is a process, part of an ongoing national conversation over German guilt and German pride which still rages several generations on. The black, red and gold may be a symbol of people power and democracy, but the very idea of patriotic flag-waving still makes many Germans feel queasy. Even now, it remains the subject of fierce debate at every World Cup or European Championship. How much patriotic fervour is appropriate, in this country of all countries? What do people really mean when they wave the national colours? And should it ever feel good to be German?

Frankfurt is as good a place as any to answer those questions. Not just the cradle of German democracy and the financial capital of Europe, it is also the place where the perpetrators of Auschwitz were first put on trial and where the great thinkers of post-war Germany tried to articulate a new kind of patriotism. It is a city with a rich Jewish history, whose modern identity is both deeply parochial and intensely international and progressive. If you want to know about Germany's complicated national identity, Frankfurt is the place to come.

Frankfurt is the only city in Germany that has proper skyscrapers: genuine Manhattan-style cloud-scratchers which are visible for miles around. In one corner of the city, there is the famous banking district, home to the headquarters of major German lenders like Commerzbank and Deutsche Bank as well as foreign banks like HSBC, ING and BNP Paribas. In the other corner, there is the new European Central Bank (ECB) building, a huge, twisted cheese grater where fiscal policy is decided on behalf of an entire continent. 'From a distance, it looks like they are miles apart, but it's actually a twenty-minute cycle,' says Matthias Thoma with a giggle. 'We are very proud of our skyline here, but it's not exactly London or New York. We are a metropolis, but a very small metropolis.'

Frankfurt is indeed a Tardis of a town, a vibrant, cosmopolitan mega-city crammed into the confines of a small regional capital. On one side of the banking district, there are the dealers and dive bars of the Bahnhofsviertel, or station quarter, which is often pigeonholed as one of the edgiest neighbourhoods in Germany.

On the other side, the historic old town slopes around the banks of the Main, its meandering alleys winding past Goethe's birth house to the Römer, the Paulskirche and the cathedral. Beyond the river in Sachsenhausen, things get a bit more medieval, with ancient restaurants serving authentic Hessian cuisine at huge wooden tables. Delicacies include pungent *Handkäs* – a hand-shaped, translucent cheese served with vinegar, raw onion and caraway seeds – and cider-like *Apfelwein* served in stone jugs known as *Bembel*.

Thoma's office lies even further south, in a stadium at the heart of a 6000-hectare city forest. A 58,000-capacity arena which has hosted everything from the World Cup to the NFL, it is officially known as the Deutsche Bank Park, though most people know it simply as the Waldstadion, or 'Forest Stadium'. For more than half a century, these woods have been home to Eintracht Frankfurt: 1959 German champions, five-time DFB-Pokal winners, three-time European finalists and the biggest club for miles around.

There are other big names in Frankfurt and the state of Hesse – FSV Frankfurt, SV Darmstadt 98, Kickers Offenbach – but none with the clout and the popularity of Eintracht. Thoma compares the club to a kind of local civic religion. 'When I was a kid growing up in the country, it was the church that bound communities together. Now it's Eintracht,' he says. 'The whole region is behind this club, and a lot of people don't come here for football, they come here for a sense of community. That means we have an enormous social responsibility.'

A bookish fifty-something with floppy brown hair, Thoma is the curator at the Eintracht Museum, one of the oldest and most successful club museums in the Bundesliga. Its permanent exhibition lies in the belly of the Waldstadion and contains everything one might expect: the 2022 Europa League trophy and the blood-stained bandage that midfielder Sebastian Rode wore in the final; old shirts, old boots, old pennants, and cups ranging from the gaudy golden DFB-Pokal to a small glass plaque from the 'Stadium Business Awards' in 2010. But Thoma's job is not just about polishing trophies. As he sees it, the museum is also a place of education. 'Obviously people come to see the trophies,' he says. 'But when they're here, maybe they also learn about people like Jule Lehmann, who played for Eintracht's third team before he was deported and disappeared without trace during the Holocaust.'

Holocaust remembrance is a major part of modern Germany. Former concentration camps like Dachau and Buchenwald are now memorial centres, while every German Chancellor since Helmut Schmidt has visited the notorious death camp at Auschwitz-Birkenau, in what is now Poland. Most German cities contain some kind of Holocaust memorial in a central location: Frankfurt's Großmarkthalle memorial lies just behind the ECB building on the edge of a major park, while Berlin's Memorial to the Murdered Jews of Europe is just a stone's throw from the Brandenburg Gate. On many German streets, there are little brass plaques built into the pavements. These *Stolpersteine*, or 'stumble stones', commemorate individual victims outside their former homes and places of work. The fact that they are mounted in the ground means you have to naturally bow your head to read them.

Yet the memorials and plaques are just the tip of the iceberg, and German remembrance culture is not just about symbolism and state visits. It is also a bottom-up process, with communities, companies and public institutions all playing a major role. From

Siemens to the Berlinale Film Festival, many major German organisations have now carried out or commissioned some kind of academic research into their own Nazi history, and football clubs like Eintracht are no different. Thoma has spent more than twenty years delving into the archives to uncover the fates of Eintracht's former Jewish members and the club's own relationship to the regime. There was a time, he says, when football shrugged its shoulders at these kinds of topics. But the more the game has become a part of mainstream society, the more clubs have stepped up to their responsibility: 'Now it's more unusual if a club isn't doing some kind of remembrance work.'

In Germany, this kind of research is often referred to as *Vergangenheitsbewältigung* or *Aufarbeitung der Vergangenheit* – both of which loosely translate as 'working through the past'. Yet even in the original German, the terms don't quite do justice to the enormity of the task. To work through something suggests that you can eventually put it behind you. And while there are some voices in Germany calling for an end to the culture of remembrance, the prevailing view is that this is an ongoing process. It is not just about remembering what happened, but making sure it never happens again. Thoma's work doesn't just involve archive research and curating exhibits, but also school projects, panel discussions with survivors, and countless other events in and around the club. 'In the end, it is mostly about reminding people that if you don't look after a democracy, things can go really, really wrong,' he says.

Football, he argues, is a good way of getting that message across and contextualising the Holocaust for a modern German audience: 'If you read about six million Jews, it just sounds like a big number. But if you read about someone's individual biography then you begin to understand.' In a game that became a mass phenomenon in the early twentieth century, there are plenty of biographies to choose from. The men who transformed an imported game into the national sport were Germans who lived through the First World War, the Weimar Republic and the rise of Nazism. And in Frankfurt as elsewhere, many of them were Jewish.

Perhaps the most famous Jewish pioneer of the German game was Walther Bensemann, who helped establish the DFB in 1900 and also founded *Kicker* magazine, which is still the country's leading football publication. Yet Bensemann was far from unique. Bayern Munich's first national successes came under Jewish president Kurt Landauer in the early 1930s, while Karlsruher FV striker Julius Hirsch was one of the German game's first national superstars. When Eintracht rose to prominence in the 1920s, they had a Jewish treasurer named Hugo Reiss, and were sponsored by the Jewish-owned local shoemaker J. & C. A. Schneider. As a result, they were known as 'the slipper-makers' and 'the Jewish boys'. As one former Eintracht player, Karl Heinemann, recalls in Thoma's book *Wir waren die Juddebube*: 'It wasn't an insult, it was just what everyone called us.'

'The Jewish population was pretty large here at that time; Frankfurt had the biggest Jewish community outside of Berlin,' explains Thoma. That is technically still true today, but the scale is much smaller. In the 1920s, the city's Jewish population was close to 30,000. In 2023, the Jewish community in Frankfurt had just over 7000 members. The difference was the 1930s. In just a few short years after the global economic crisis of 1929, Adolf Hitler's Nazi Party went from being fringe extremists to a major electoral force. By 1932, they had become the largest party in parliament, and at the end of January 1933 they wrested control of government. They quickly set about dismantling the democratic Weimar Republic and establishing a totalitarian state in its place. Hitler was named Führer in 1934, giving him free rein to implement his racist ideology as dictator.

'Pretty much all the major German clubs brought themselves into line relatively quickly,' says Thoma. As early as April 1933, the DFB was urging its clubs to remove Jewish members from positions of influence. DFB founder Bensemann fled to Switzerland in March 1933, leaving *Kicker* to become a willing mouthpiece for Nazi propaganda. Landauer, who would later lose all four of his siblings to the Holocaust, stepped down as Bayern president around the same time. Eintracht treasurer Reiss also resigned in early 1933, and later fled to South America. His parents were one of the many Frankfurt Jews deported to the Lodz ghetto, where they later died. The Nuremberg race laws that underpinned the systematic exclusion of Jews from public life would not come into force until two years later, and yet most historians agree that football did little to resist this process in the spring of 1933. Thoma notes that there is anecdotal evidence to suggest that Eintracht attempted to help some of their former Jewish members long into the 1930s, but he is wary of making too much of it.

'We can't use that to clean our image, and it is also important that we don't allow ourselves to be painted as the victims. The fact we were a club with many Jewish members doesn't mean we don't bear responsibility for what happened: that's an important thing to get across to people,' he says. Eintracht, after all, were complicit in the expulsion of Jewish members, many of whom did not survive the Shoah, and it also counted plenty of perpetrators among its ranks. The club's wartime chairman Rudolf Gramlich would later oversee some of their greatest successes as president, including their title win in 1959 and the famous European Cup final against Real Madrid in 1960. Only after his death did it emerge that Gramlich had also profited from the expropriation of Jewish businesses, served in the SS, and was potentially implicated in war crimes. In 2018, Eintracht launched an extensive investigation into his past and in 2020, they officially removed his honorary presidency. 'Obviously that happened too late, but it is still good that it happened,' says Thoma.

Football was not alone in that regard. Even in wider society, German remembrance culture did not develop overnight. In the immediate years after the war, there was little appetite to face up to the horrors of the Holocaust. In 1945, the surviving Nazi top brass were convicted at the Nuremberg trials, but with many Germans still fighting to survive in the post-war devastation, attempts to educate the public about the extent of the genocide had only limited success. Likewise, the Allies' 'denazification' programmes, which sought to identify and convict those most complicit in the regime, were quickly overshadowed by the need to build West Germany into a strong Cold War ally. Gramlich was far from the only committed Nazi who slipped through the gaps, and the first two decades after the war were largely characterised by a desire to move on, rather than look back. It wasn't until 1963, the year the Bundesliga was founded, that the first trial against personnel from the Auschwitz extermination camp took place on German soil.

That trial was held in Frankfurt, and it began in the chamber of the city parliament in the Römer city hall, just a stone's throw from the Paulskirche. Where once German democracy had taken its first steps, it now began to face the horrors that had emerged from its own collapse. Twenty-two individuals were convicted at the three Frankfurt trials between 1963 and 1968, with many of them serving life sentences. Perhaps most importantly, the court cases also thrust the shocking details of the Shoah into the public eye. The trials were not only covered in the media, but also prompted a wide range of intellectual and artistic responses. The initial reluctance to face up to the genocide was now being challenged by a new generation of Germans, one which was unburdened by direct involvement in the crimes.

With a bit of distance, the country was finally asking itself the most fundamental question: what does it mean to be German after Auschwitz? In the early 1950s, Frankfurt philosophers like Theodor W. Adorno had tackled the Holocaust as a question of cultural theory, famously stating that 'to write poetry after Auschwitz is barbaric'. With the Auschwitz trials, a much more accessible debate began to unfold about responsibility for the genocide. The 1968 student movement in particular would launch scathing attacks on the West German establishment, pointing to the Nazi past of many leading politicians, academics and cultural figures. The debates continued unabated into the 1980s, when conservative and left-wing intellectuals clashed over the issue of German guilt and the singularity of the Holocaust. Thinkers like Jürgen Habermas, Adorno's successor at the Frankfurt Institute for Social Research, would ultimately argue that Germany could never embrace a conventional national identity based on flags, myths, poems and heroes. If Germans were patriotic, it had to be 'constitutional patriotism', a pride in democratic values and institutions.

That kind of post-national thinking still has a profound effect on German society today. 'Everyone wants to be proud of where they come from, but a lot of people are very wary of national patriotism here in Germany, so regional patriotism is much more comfortable,' says Thoma. 'If you walk around Frankfurt nowadays, you see all these things like Bembels and Apfelwein glasses which used to be functional items and are now a part of people's identity.'

Not that you have to drink Apfelwein from a Bembel. You can also buy it in an Eintracht-branded can from the local kiosk. Football fandom, after all, is the ultimate exercise in regional patriotism, and German football culture also reflects a tendency towards the regional, rather than the national. While German club football has one of the most vibrant fan cultures in the world, that doesn't necessarily translate at international level. Unlike in England or Italy, club fans rarely display the national colours alongside those of their own team, and support for the national team is generally far more muted. A YouGov survey in 2023 found that almost two-thirds of Germans claimed to have no interest in the Germany men's team at all.

That was partly down to recent results, with Germany having crashed out in the early rounds of every major tournament from 2018 to 2022. Yet it also reflects a certain shyness when it comes to supporting a team that still plays in the black and white colours of imperial Prussia. The horrors of history still weigh heavy on Germany, and there are many who take more pride in being a Frankfurter, a European or a democrat than being a German. It isn't that Germany doesn't do national patriotism at all. But it is always complicated. And even in football, it takes something pretty special to get all of Germany waving the flag.

Markus Stenger was thirty years old when the World Cup came to Germany in 2006, and as a DFB employee, he was one of the lucky few who experienced the tournament live in the stadiums. 'The weather was great, the atmosphere was great, the football was great,' he says. 'I only have positive memories of it, and that's also the nice thing about that World Cup. There were no smartphones and no Instagram then, so it's one of the last tournaments that largely just exists in our memories.'

Eighteen years later, Stenger is now the man tasked with making new memories. Now in his late forties, he is the managing director of the Euro 2024 GmbH, the UEFA and DFB joint venture in charge of organising the European Championships. He meets me at the tournament headquarters at Frankfurt's Otto-Fleck-Schneise, a sprawling complex of mid-century offices nestled in the woods behind the Waldstadion. Originally built ahead of the 1974 World Cup in West Germany, this site served as the DFB's headquarters for fifty years until the federation opened a new modern campus up the road in 2022. Now, the walls are plastered with official Euro 2024 branding. This will be the first major tournament Germany has hosted since 2006, and alongside tournament director and former Germany captain Philipp Lahm, Stenger is hoping to recreate some of the magic of that hot, heady summer.

2006 was a watershed moment for Germany, a tournament that seared itself indelibly into the country's collective memory. The post-reunification recession of the 1990s had come and gone, and the global financial crisis of 2008 was yet to hit. Optimism abounded, and amid record summer temperatures, the world's football fans descended on Germany for one of the biggest festivals the country had ever seen. The national team cast off their old reputation for grim, destructive efficiency, and swept into the semi-finals with free-flowing football. The population embraced the party atmosphere, flocking in their thousands to watch the games on big screens at the newly invented 'fan miles'. 'There was definitely a feeling that we had never felt before,' says Stenger. 'Everyone was on the street, it was fantastic. And that rubbed off on all the visitors to the country too. They were saying: "Hey, Germany is actually a cool place to come to."'

As well as changing Germany's image abroad, 2006 also led to a shift in the country's own idea of itself. As thousands of people waved German flags in the street and hailed their losing semi-finalists as heroes, there was a sense that something had shifted in the German psyche. Germans had waved flags in the street before, but this was not a single, localised moment of spontaneous national euphoria like the fall of the Wall or the 1990 victory celebrations at the Römer. This was a whole summer, and the flag was everywhere. As the then German President Horst Köhler put it: 'I am no longer the only one with the black, red and gold flying on my car.'

It wasn't just that everyone was flying the flag, adds Stenger, but also that the flag seemed for once to be flying for everyone. In the 2000s, new, more liberal citizenship laws and a shift in policy at the DFB meant that the national team was becoming more representative of the diversity in German society. The 2006 squad contained players of Ghanaian descent like Gerald Asamoah and David Odonkor, while players like Mesut Özil and Sami Khedira were emerging in the national youth teams. 'Even some of my Turkish friends, who hadn't ever felt represented by the national team before, suddenly felt it was something they belonged to as well,' says Stenger, who had spent most of his adult life in international, multicultural Frankfurt. Rather than something dangerous or chauvinistic, German pride suddenly felt good, inclusive and progressive.

Six months later, that feeling was immortalised in a documentary film on public TV entitled *Deutschland: Ein Sommermärchen ('Germany: A Summer Fairytale')*. The title was a reference to a nineteenth-century Heinrich Heine poem which poked fun at schmaltzy German nationalism, but filmmaker Sönke Wortmann arguably did the opposite, casting the tournament as a sun-drenched moment of national joy and togetherness. The idea stuck, and 'summer fairytale' has been a byword for the 2006 World Cup ever since. This was not just a football tournament. It was a moment in which a traumatised country came together like never before, and for once seemed entirely at ease with itself. 'That is the power that big tournaments can have,' says Stenger.

Yet in 2023, the optimism of 2006 feels a long way away, and Stenger admits that not everyone shares his belief in the power of major tournaments. Many Germans now see major sporting events as an expensive extravagance, and recent referendums in Munich and Hamburg have seen voters emphatically reject potential Olympic bids. Recent major football tournaments, meanwhile, have had a tendency to divide people as much as unite them. As in other Western European countries, the World Cups in Russia and Qatar were deeply controversial among German football fans, with most ultra groups and several hundred sports bars supporting a campaign to boycott the latter.

Even the summer fairytale has lost some of its shine. In 2015, an investigation by *Der Spiegel* reported suspicions of bribery and corruption in Germany's bid to host the 2006 World Cup. The allegations led to legal investigations in both Switzerland

and Germany, and the DFB has been in a state of permacrisis ever since. Between 2015 and 2021, the federation saw three consecutive presidents step down in disgrace. The first, Wolfgang Niersbach, resigned over the fallout from the *Spiegel* report. The second, Reinhard Grindel, stepped down in 2019 over a scandal involving a luxury watch, after spending months mired in a racism row. The third, Fritz Keller, left after it emerged he had compared his deputy to a notorious Nazi-era judge. Germany's miserable performances at the 2018 and 2022 World Cups only increased the pressure on the federation, while in 2020, its headquarters were raided by the German tax authorities. I ask Stenger whether Euro 2024 was an opportunity for the DFB to win back trust. 'It isn't just an opportunity, it is *the* opportunity,' he says.

At the same time, there are some who have begun to revisit the legacy of the 2006 World Cup. Critics of the 'summer fairytale' narrative argue that it didn't promote constitutional patriotism or inclusive civic nationalism, but simply brought a more visceral, flag-waving style of patriotism back into the German mainstream. Clemens Heni, an academic at the Berlin International Center for the Study of Antisemitism, even went as far as to argue that the World Cup had led directly to the rise of far-right parties like the AfD, which was founded in 2013 and won 12.6 per cent of votes at the 2017 election. 'The World Cup wasn't a sporting event, it was an event of German nationalism,' Heni told the *Frankfurter Rundschau* in 2019.

Sitting with Stenger in the Euro 2024 headquarters, it is clear that this tournament is being framed differently. Rather than using the national colours like many host nations do, the German organisers have designed a logo that is a collage of a dozen different European flags. The tournament slogan is 'United by football – in the heart of Europe', and its visual identity is based around a plain European blue. 'It's a European championship, not a German one,' says Stenger.

He doesn't put it more explicitly than that, but the emphasis on the European feels like more than a simple marketing decision. European integration has always been a fundamental pillar of the post-war political consensus in Germany and is seen by many as a bulwark against resurgent German nationalism. The commitment to the European project is written into the constitution of the Federal Republic, and polls consistently show that around seventy-five per cent of Germans think the country has a brighter future within the EU. 'I'm not necessarily a fan of all the bureaucracy in Brussels, but I was so sad when Britain left the EU,' says Stenger. 'For me, Europe means being able to travel freely, not having borders, learning about other cultures and being open to one another. It's about thinking beyond borders.'

He is not the only one striking this tone. In early 2023, tournament director Philipp Lahm said in an interview with German news agency DPA that Euro 2024 should be 'a festival of togetherness which strengthens Europe'. A few months later, he wrote an op-ed in *Kicker* declaring that 'this tournament should be a call to solidarity and a restrengthening of the European idea'. As a player, Lahm scored the opening goal of the 2006 World Cup, and at times, it has felt like he is on a one-man mission to save Europe with another football fairytale.

Stenger is a little more equivocal. 'In 2006, we were all quite surprised at how easy-going everything felt. Given the geopolitical situation at the moment, I'm not sure people will be able to have the same feeling this time,' he admits. The Covid-19 pandemic, the wars in Ukraine and the Middle East and the resulting energy and inflation crises have all caused as much anxiety in Germany as elsewhere, and it is hard to imagine a return to the wild optimism of 2006, regardless of what flag people are waving.

Yet for all the difficulties of the last few years, he remains convinced that big tournaments can change society and football can make the case for a European, progressive and tolerant Germany. 'Euro 2024 should be a bit like Frankfurt: international and open,' he says. 'Everyone should come as they are and see that, in Germany, you can be exactly who you want to be, regardless of your gender, your religion or who you love. That hasn't always been the case, and we all need to work extremely hard to make sure it remains that way.'

More than 500 kilometres away in Berlin, Omid Nouripour is also making the case for an open, democratic Germany. 'We have an amazing strength in this country,' he says. 'Our democracy is so much stronger than people sometimes make out, and we can't let ourselves be drowned out by the people who are actively opposing our constitution.'

Nouripour knows the state of German democracy better than most – he is one of two Bundestag MPs for the city of Frankfurt and the co-chair of the German Green Party. When we speak in autumn 2023, his party are in government alongside the neo-liberal Free Democratic Party (FDP) and Olaf Scholz's centre-left Social Democrats (SPD). The 'traffic-light government' (so-called for the parties' red, green and yellow colours) is the first three-party coalition at national level since the 1950s, and it has been a bumpy ride so far. The FDP and the Greens in particular are not natural bedfellows, and the government has been beset by internal division over everything from nuclear power to the speed limit. As co-leader of his party, Nouripour is one of those charged with hashing out laborious compromises in torturous backroom negotiations. There are some issues, however, on which he will not budge.

'There is only one club's flag allowed on this desk,' he declares at the beginning of the interview, plonking a little Eintracht Frankfurt flag down on the table in front of him.

In Nouripour's Berlin office, Eintracht are everywhere. On one wall, there is a poster from the European Cup semi-final win over Rangers in 1960 and a framed photograph of the title-winning team of 1959. Hanging from the door of the cupboard in the corner is a scarf from the 2022 Europa League final. Even his campaign posters include a nod to the football club. The word *Eintracht* literally means 'harmony' or 'unity' in German, and Nouripour's election slogan is *Eintracht und Frieden*: 'harmony and peace'. He is probably the most powerful football fan in the country, and in nearly two decades as a Bundestag MP, he has brought football right into the heart of the German parliament.

In 2012, Nouripour founded the EFC bundesAdler, the first ever official parliamentary fan club of a Bundesliga team. The group, he says proudly, now number around one hundred members, including civil servants, serving MPs and former and current cabinet ministers. It also covers almost the entire political spectrum, from the centre-right CDU to the hard-left Linke party. 'We don't always agree on everything,' he admits. 'When we go to the stadium, there is always a disagreement about whether to go on the terraces or in the VIP seats. And of course, there are a few members of our group who want to sit as far apart from each other as possible. But the bottom line is that we come together, we talk about politics, and we watch football. And when Eintracht win, we all hug each other.'

German lawmakers are not known for their displays of unbridled emotion. But that, Nouripour insists, is the magic of Eintracht. Football tribalism can bring even the most embittered political rivals together, and the fan club is also an exercise in finding common ground and promoting cross-party cooperation. 'The democratic parties have so much in common and we need to work across boundaries on a lot of issues: the decarbonisation of our industries, support of Ukraine, social justice, and the defence of constitutional democracy,' says Nouripour.

At the time he is talking in October 2023, there is plenty of concern about the strength of German democracy. A few days earlier, the far-right AfD made huge gains in state elections, overtaking the Greens in both Bavaria and Nouripour's home state of Hesse. The AfD are the only party not represented in the Eintracht fan club, and when Nouripour talks about the 'democratic parties', he means everyone but them. Their rise is part of a global trend towards nativist politics, and as of 2024, they are not yet as strong as equivalent parties in Italy, Hungary or even France. But in a country like Germany, the resurgence of the far right is always more alarming than elsewhere. Their critics see the AfD party not just as an opponent, but as an existential threat to German democracy. In 2022, the domestic intelligence agency BfV officially classified the party as a 'suspected threat' to the constitutional order.

Many of the AfD's policies would, until recently, have been unthinkable in German politics. What began as a fringe anti-Euro protest party in 2013 has since morphed into a major electoral force, which campaigns on an anti-immigration platform with strong veins of Islamophobia, climate change denial, and apologism for Putin's Russia. They have also launched sustained attacks on Germany's culture of atonement for Nazi crimes. In 2018, their then leader Alexander Gauland described the Nazi era as a mere 'speck of birdshit' in German history. His more radical party colleague Björn Höcke has referred to the Berlin Holocaust Memorial as a 'monument of disgrace' and called for a '180-degree turn' in German remembrance culture.

Much of this is a direct challenge to Germany's entire postwar political consensus. At the Reichstag parliament building in Berlin, notes Nouripour, MPs still walk past graffiti left by Red Army soldiers three-quarters of a century earlier. This is a country where the self-inflicted scars of war and genocide are still raw, and Holocaust remembrance doesn't just shape Germany's society and cultural life, but also its very idea of nationhood. When naturalised Germans obtain citizenship, they explicitly commit to Germany's responsibility for Nazi crimes and 'the protection of Jewish life'. The same idea also informs many of Germany's most fundamental foreign policy dogmas, from its commitment to the security of Israel to its dedication to the European project. The limits of those positions are occasionally tested: in late 2023, Germany faced criticism both internally and externally for its reluctance to back calls for a ceasefire in Gaza. Yet there are good reasons why responsibility for the Holocaust still looms large in modern politics. More than just a superficial guilt complex, it is part of the very foundation of the country's democratic culture. 'Our constitution was based on the lessons of the Shoah, and that is a good thing,' says Nouripour.

Yet the past doesn't make Germany immune to right-wing extremism, and the rise of the AfD is just one of several worrying developments. Official figures have shown a rise in incidents of far-right violence over the last decade or so,[8] including shocking, deadly attacks on Jewish and immigrant communities. In 2019, nine people were killed in a racist shooting in Hanau, just outside Frankfurt. In the same year, a gunman killed two people while attempting to attack a synagogue in Halle on Yom Kippur. The far right have also exploited public unease over Covid lockdowns, immigration and in particular the arrival of those fleeing war in countries like Syria. In 2015, when the German asylum system struggled to manage the arrival of more than a million refugees in a single year, Islamophobic street movements like Pegida mobilised thousands of protesters in cities across the country.

At times, it can feel like the problems run deep into the mainstream. Astonishingly, it is still not unheard of for white comedians to black up and use the N-word on primetime German television, and while German conservatives often slam Muslim communities for not assimilating, many of Germany's Muslims have long faced significant structural hurdles to integration. Until Nouripour's government changed the citizenship laws in 2024, it was almost impossible to hold dual German and Turkish nationality beyond the age of eighteen. For those born in Germany but descended from Turkish *Gastarbeiter*, that meant a stark choice between the country they were born in and that of their immediate family. In recent years, the public discourse around such issues has arguably only become more coarse, more polarised.

In football, that became painfully clear around the 2018 World Cup. Before the tournament began, Germany players Mesut Özil and Ilkay Gündogan accepted an invitation to meet with Turkish President Recep Tayyip Erdoğan and were both photographed handing him a signed shirt. For many of their critics, the issue was simply that they had met an autocratic leader in the middle of a controversial Turkish election campaign. Yet inevitably, the saga also prompted a ferocious debate about race, identity and split loyalties in the Turkish-German community. When Germany crashed out in the group stage of the World Cup, Özil promptly retired from the German national team, claiming he had been made a scapegoat for the team's failure because of his background. 'In the eyes of some people, I am a German when the team wins, and an immigrant when we lose,' he said.

Nouripour, who was born in Tehran and moved to Frankfurt as child when his parents fled conflict and repression in Iran, is all too familiar with the racism in German society. As one of the few high-profile Muslim politicians in Germany, he receives a constant barrage of hate speech and aggression, which he talks about with an impressive, if slightly weary, levity. 'It was only when I saw my colleague Cem Özdemir speaking on television in the early 1990s that I realised you didn't have to be called Karl-Heinz to be a German politician,' he quips at one point, adding that when he first started out in politics, he initially looked into joining both the Greens and the Social Democrats. 'I decided for the Greens in the end, because they were the only ones who didn't ask me where I came from.'

Ultimately, though, Nouripour is an optimist. He speaks passionately about the 'amazing strength' of German civil society, and points to the thousands of people engaged in volunteering work across the country. His own biography, he insists, is proof that Germany is also a 'special' country. 'There aren't many other places in the world where someone with my background could have the opportunities I have had,' he says, adding that the increasing fragmentation of society is not inexorable. 'It isn't a law of nature that everything just gets coarser and wilder and more polarised. It's in our hands to push it in a different direction.'

Perhaps unsurprisingly, he holds up Eintracht as a good example of how to do so. 'Frankfurt and the surrounding area is a region that has people from so many different walks of life, but somehow everyone finds a place at Eintracht,' he says. He puts that down in large part to the leadership of one man in particular. Peter Fischer, who served as Eintracht president from 2000 to 2024, is one of the most charismatic club directors in German football. A notorious bon vivant who slurps apple wine from trophies and buys beers for fans on away trips, he is also a fiercely outspoken critic of the AfD and is a committed anti-racism campaigner. After the Hanau attack in 2019, he appeared on stage at a vigil to express Eintracht's solidarity with the family of the victims. Two years earlier, he told *FAZ* newspaper that 'voting for the AfD is irreconcilable with the values in our club statutes, so if you are an Eintracht member, you can't vote AfD.'

The comments drew howls of indignation from the far-right party itself and were to some extent a genuine political risk on Fischer's part. Yet his tough words went down well, and Fischer was confirmed as president with over ninety-nine per cent of the vote a few years later. 'I don't know a single civil society actor who is more outspoken on the AfD than Peter Fischer,' says Nouripour with audible admiration. That's important, he adds, because football has a far greater ability to bring people together against hate than politicians do. 'If I tell people the

Green Party co-chairman Omid Nouripour sits in the Waldstadion in Frankfurt. © Victor Martini/Bündnis90 Die Grünen

AfD are bad, then people will quite rightly say I have a vested interest because they got more votes than us at the last regional elections. If Peter Fischer says it, it's different. That's why football clubs are so important.'

We are back to the idea of football clubs as modern-day churches, as places where people come together across economic and cultural backgrounds to find some kind of shared identity. That is particularly true in Germany, where football fans play such an active role in club life and regional identities are so strong. In 2006, many hoped that something similar was happening around the national team, but perhaps they were always barking up the wrong tree. In Germany, national identity alone will never quite cut it.

Back at the Römer city hall in Frankfurt, there are three flags that hang from the famous balcony. The black, red and gold of the 1848 national assembly hangs in the middle, with the red eagle of Frankfurt to its right and the blue and yellow standard of the European Union to its left. This is Frankfurt: birthplace of German democracy, regional capital, and seat of European finance. Yet it is also the success model of modern Germany: a nation state, but one where the dangers of nationalism are always checked by the regional federal states within and the European community without. 'The prosperity and peace we have had in the last seventy years are an exceptional thing which would never have been possible without European integration,' says Nouripour. 'That's especially true for a country that was the cause of so much destruction under the Nazis.'

For seventy years, the model has worked. Yet with the AfD on the rise and the horrors of Nazism beginning to fade from living memory, the fight to keep fascism at bay remains as relevant as ever. And there is one city in particular where that fight takes place on the football terraces.

HAMBURG

6

HAMBURG
POLITICAL FOOTBALL

It is derby day in Hamburg, and for once it isn't raining. Germany's most northerly major city lies just sixty-eight miles upriver from the North Sea, and it usually pays to bring an umbrella. But today, the sky is clear. At the Jungfernstieg waterfront in the city centre, the Alster shimmers in the afternoon sun, and the punters in the cafés pick idly at their glasses of ice cream. If it weren't for the football fans, it would be almost idyllic.

Instead, the air is crackling. It is a few hours until kick-off, and a crowd of St. Pauli fans are slowly beginning to annex the promenade, flooding it in a sea of brown, white and black. The city has seemed distracted all day, and now the anticipation is slowly turning into nerves. The sticker wars have been ratcheted up a notch, the scarves are coming out, and people are beginning to bristle at the sight of the wrong colours. There are no compromises on a day like this, no sitting on the fence. You are in one camp or the other. Home or away. Us or them. HSV or St. Pauli. St. Pauli or HSV.

Later, at HSV's Volksparkstadion, the fireworks begin in earnest. The first flares go off as the HSV players come out to warm up, and the first rocket sails out of the block after just twelve minutes. At the start of the second half, huge clouds of black, white and blue smoke billow out from the home end and a volley of crackers cut through it into the sky. Even in the posh seats, veins and vocal chords strain with the adrenalin of it all. The game itself is also gut-churning, tossed this way and that as the two teams flail around in the emotional currents. St. Pauli take the lead and have the wind in their sails, before HSV seize the rudder and fight back to lead 3–1. At one point, the TV cameras settle on HSV coach Tim Walter. He is staring into his own lap with his hands behind his head, looking like a man coming to terms with the firing squad. When the whistle goes, it is 4–3 to HSV, and the stadium explodes once again.

There are other derbies in German football: rivalries that are older, more violent, more relentlessly hyped. Yet across the length and breadth of the country, there is arguably no fixture that captures the imagination quite like this one. No city feud that has such vivid, relatable characters, or such obvious cultural resonance. In Hamburg, football is not just football. It is identity politics, ideology, class war. And on the face of it at least, the roles are clear cut.

HSV (Ha-Ess-Fow) are the *ancien régime*, part of German football's traditional establishment. Their roll of honour includes national heroes such as Uwe Seeler and international stars like Kevin Keegan, and they have amassed an impressive cabinet of crown jewels over the years: as of 2024, they are six-time national champions, three-time DFB-Pokal winners and one of only three German clubs ever to have won the European Cup. Relegation in 2018 may have robbed them of some of their old majesty, but like Cologne or Stuttgart, HSV still have pretensions to absolute rule in their city. Their name, Hamburger Sport-Verein, says it all. Their slogan, 'Only HSV', hammers the point home.

FC St. Pauli, by contrast, are the pirates of the port city, the rebel club more famous for their politics than their football. In terms of on-field success, they have contributed very little to Hamburg's footballing history. But the left-wing, anti-fascist leanings of both the club and its supporters have made them famous across the world. At every home game, the skull and crossbones of the Jolly Roger flies over the entrance of the stadium, while the image of Che Guevara waves proudly in the home end. This is punk rock football, football as revolution.

The two clubs could hardly be more different, and yet they are both icons of their home city. Hamburg is a port town, and like all port towns, it contains multitudes. Centuries of trade have brought wealth, power, snobbery and status, but also diversity, counterculture, grime and grit. On the one hand, there is the proud old Hanseatic merchant city, which was once the epicentre of European trade and is still the continent's third-biggest trading port; the city that gave Germany its most influential media mogul in Axel Springer, and one of its most important post-war Chancellors in Helmut Schmidt. On the other hand, there is the Hamburg of St. Pauli and the Reeperbahn, a town of radicalism and ill repute which is home to one of the most famous red-light districts outside of Amsterdam and one of the biggest left-wing autonomist scenes in Europe. In this Hamburg, politics takes place not in the halls of power, but out on the streets.

On some level, that is a duality which speaks to all Germans, even those outside of Hamburg. Germany's post-war political story has always been a conversation between the radicals and the moderates, the establishment and the extremes. As a rule of thumb, German politics tend towards consensus and continuity (three of the Federal Republic's nine Chancellors since 1949 have served for fourteen years or more). Yet the country has also been shaped by more radically progressive movements, from the student revolutionaries of 1968 to modern-day environmental activists like Last Generation and Extinction Rebellion. Ask a neutral German football fan which Hamburg team they prefer, and you might get some inkling about their general world view.

HSV or St. Pauli? Establishment or underdog? Compromise and consensus or radicalism and revolution? This is a derby that makes a mockery of the old adage that football and politics don't mix. In Hamburg, football is always political. But in football, as in real life, there is more than one way to do politics.

The Millerntor stadium lies in the shadow of a Nazi-era bunker. Behind the away fans in the north stand, the huge concrete behemoth towers over the stadium, forty metres high with walls almost four metres thick. Built by forced labourers in 1942 to defend against Allied air raids, it was deemed too large to be demolished after the war ended. So it stayed put, a militaristic eyesore on the skyline and an enduring warning from the darkest period of German history. At the Millerntor, they take that warning seriously. Looming over the terraces on the western stand of the stadium, there are four words daubed in huge, white block capitals on a red background:

Kein Fussball den Faschisten. No football for fascists.

FC St. Pauli are not the only anti-fascist football club in Europe. From Bohemians in Dublin to Rayo Vallecano in

'No football for fascists': At St. Pauli's Millerntor stadium, the club's politics are on full display © FCSP

Madrid, there are other clubs with famously left-wing fan-bases, and others who take pride in their stands against racism, homophobia and discrimination. Yet there is nowhere quite like St. Pauli, where progressive politics are such an essential part of the club's identity. From the terraces to the boardroom, this is a club that defines itself by its political convictions. Since they were founded in 1910, St. Pauli have spent only eight seasons in the national top flight and have never won a major trophy. But with their politics, their fans and their unofficial skull and crossbones logo, they have achieved a fame which most German clubs can only dream of. St. Pauli are an icon of modern football, and the world's quintessential left-wing cult club.

'I prefer to use the term "progressive" rather than "left-wing", because in terms of party politics, we are obviously neutral. But we do believe that everything in football is political, whether it's a World Cup in Qatar or fighting discrimination in the stadium,' says Sven Brux, St. Pauli's long-time head of security. The slogan painted on the terraces, he explains, is a variation on the old German antifa motto *Kein Fußbreit den Faschisten*, meaning 'Don't give the fascists an inch.' All St. Pauli have done is apply that to football: 'If you're against Nazis in real life, then you should be against Nazis in the stadium too.'

Brux is a towering warhorse of a man with an interrogatory stare, a pierced left ear and a warm, toothy grin. Few know the club better than he does, and few have done more to shape its political identity. St. Pauli were not always the left-wing club they are today, and Brux was one of the first generation of fans who brought punk and politics to the terraces in the 1980s. He has since become a club legend in his own right, serving as fan liaison officer, head of security and director of matchday organisation. He is also the co-founder of the Jolly Roger, the famous matchday boozer which lies just over the road from the Millerntor. Like the stadium itself, the pub is a place that nails its colours to the mast. The facade is covered from top to bottom in a thick layer of stickers, and a huge three-dimensional St. Pauli emblem hangs in the window. Inside, the air is thick with stale beer, smoke and sweat, and a DJ booth at the back blasts out punk and ska classics. The beer is Astra, the famous Hamburg brand with the stubby brown bottles and the heart-shaped anchor, and even the wine comes in bottles labelled 'Not for Fascists'. This is St. Pauli. It is not a place of half measures.

The football club takes its name from a district that lies to the west of Hamburg city centre, just outside the old city walls. It stretches from the Millerntor at the top of the hill in the northeast down to the St. Pauli piers on the banks of the Elbe, where steamships used to refuel and the tour boats now compete for custom among the souvenir shops and the fish-sandwich vendors. St. Pauli is one of Hamburg's great attractions, a party neighbourhood par excellence which ranks among the most famous red-light districts in the world. Sex work, which is legal and regulated in Germany, still dominates the main strip around the Reeperbahn thoroughfare, but St. Pauli is about more than just brothels and sex shops. *Der Kiez*, as locals call it, is a cacophony of theatres, music venues, cinemas and dive bars. Along with the St. Georg district to the east, it is a bastion of Hamburg's LGBTQI scene and a place that has enchanted artists and musicians for decades. The Beatles gigged at St. Pauli's Star Club early in their careers. Tom Waits penned a haunting ode to the seediness of the Reeperbahn. West German rocker Udo Lindenberg lovingly referred to it as 'my old gangster bride'. 'The sea-faring history meant that this was always a melting pot, a place for outlaws and oddballs of all kinds,' says Brux.

He himself moved to St. Pauli from Cologne in the mid-1980s, at a time when the neighbourhood was changing dramatically. The global economic crises of the 1970s had hit the port city hard, gang wars had begun to break out in the red-light district, and the area was emptying out. 'A lot of the shipyard workers had gone by the 1980s, and there were a lot of houses standing around empty and unrenovated,' says Brux. 'You started to get an alternative scene moving in, securing the cheap living space and starting their own pubs, their own venues, their own part of town.'

That 'alternative scene' was just one of many left-wing movements which had emerged from the political explosion of 1968. After the student protests had run their course in the late 1960s, some of the activists went into mainstream politics, joining establishment parties like the SPD. Others took a more radical path: in the 1970s, the left-wing terrorist group Red Army Faction (RAF) unleashed a wave of political violence against the West German state, killing police officers, diplomats, state prosecutors and US military personnel. At the same time, peaceful anti-nuclear protests mobilised hundreds of thousands to the streets from 1979 onwards, playing a significant role in the birth of the German Green Party in 1980. In the major cities, meanwhile, leftist squatters began to occupy empty buildings in run-down, underpopulated areas like St. Pauli in Hamburg and Kreuzberg in West Berlin, setting up artists' collectives, anarchist communes and self-governed 'autonomous centres' which rejected the authority of the state and the market. 'St. Pauli was like an oasis,' says Brux, who came to Hamburg to do national service in a local sailors' hostel rather than serve in the military. 'You could create your own world.'

In Hamburg, that world centred around twelve nineteenth-century townhouses on Hafenstraße, a residential promenade between the Reeperbahn and the St. Pauli piers. The buildings were abandoned and billed for demolition when squatters moved into them in the early 1980s, and they soon became the beating heart of St. Pauli's new, autonomous left-wing scene. Over the following decade, the city's attempts to evict them were met with protests and violent clashes with police. At the high point of the tensions in autumn 1987, Hafenstraße was the biggest news story in the country as the squatters erected makeshift barricades from furniture, upturned vehicles and barbed wire, and around five thousand police officers were put on standby to storm the buildings. As potentially deadly clashes loomed, a last-minute deal was struck which allowed the squatters to stay.

At that point, FC St. Pauli still had little to do with these revolutionaries on the other side of the Kiez. Football, notes Brux,

Residents clear the barricades after the showdown with police at the Hafenstraße squats in 1987. © dpa Picture-Alliance/Alamy Stock Photo

was generally a 'no-go' for punks and leftists in the 1980s, with right-wing violence rife in stadiums across West Germany and the rest of Europe. HSV's fanbase was one of many that had notorious far-right elements, and hooligans would sporadically descend on Hafenstraße spoiling for a fight. St. Pauli, meanwhile, were not the club they are today. After a brief spell of success in the 1950s, they had long since retreated into the shadow of HSV, and by the 1980s, they were at their lowest ebb. Financial problems briefly pushed them as low as the third tier and attendances dwindled to just a few thousand. Brux was one of a few punks who would occasionally go along to games, but at that time, they were still in a minority. 'It was a normal club back then, with normal fans: lots of old dockworkers and people like that,' he says. 'The punks had our spot behind the dugout, but there were only a hundred or so of us at most.'

But that was about to change. In November 1987, just two days after the showdown at Hafenstraße, St. Pauli beat SSV Ulm 4–3 at the Millerntor, launching a nine-game unbeaten run at home in the second division. A few months later, they were promoted back to the Bundesliga for the first time in more than a decade. Buoyed by their newfound success, the club directors soon announced plans to transform the club's intimate stadium into a so-called 'Sport Dome', a futuristic arena complete with an attached hotel, shopping mall and congress centre. The idea sparked outrage among fans, and it was the punks who led the protests. Suddenly, Hafenstraße squatters who had been on the barricades just two years earlier were marching alongside football fans. 'We came from a scene that was politically organised by definition, so we knew how to get a demonstration off the ground, distribute leaflets and stuff like that,' says Brux. Within weeks, they had persuaded the club to shelve the Sport Dome plans.

The protests sparked a chain reaction which would eventually turn the football club into a left-wing icon. In the coming years, the punks became more and more involved with the St. Pauli fan scene. They founded the *Millerntor Roar*, one of the first major fanzines in German football, and opened the *Fanladen*, a community centre near the ground which held supporter events and sold home-made merchandise. They started producing stickers with a St. Pauli logo next to a fist smashing a swastika, and co-opted the Jolly Roger as a new unofficial symbol on flags and t-shirts. They also began to get involved in fan politics, pressuring the club on issues like racism and ticket prices. All of it was an extension of the same DIY political activism that had saved the Millerntor. 'The right-wingers always accused us of having some kind of masterplan to start a political revolution through football. In reality, we just went to the stadium to get drunk, and then reacted to the political realities we saw there,' says Brux. He quotes Ulrike Meinhof, one of the co-founders of the Red Army Faction. 'Protest means saying you disagree with something. Resistance means stopping it from happening.'

In purely footballing terms, however, Brux and his contemporaries had started a revolution. Just as Hafenstraße became a blueprint for other endangered squats across Germany, so the St. Pauli fans had unleashed a new idea of fan politics in German football. In Hamburg, many HSV fans who had become disillusioned by violence and racism on the terraces began to drift towards St. Pauli instead. And elsewhere in the country, other left-wing fans began to adopt them as their team or else copy the Kiez club's methods. The design of St. Pauli's anti-Nazi stickers is now used by fans across Germany, while organised supporter demonstrations are a regular feature of the modern German game. At a time when German fan culture was still dominated by right-wing hooliganism, St. Pauli offered an alternative vision. Still today, the club's official slogan is 'Another Football is Possible'.

Nowadays, though, St. Pauli face a different set of challenges. Brux became fan liaison officer in 1989, and in the years that followed, more and more people from the leftist scene would take on positions of influence at the club. 'When Oke Göttlich became president in 2014, it was like we had come full circle. I remember him standing with us on the terraces as a young lad,' says Brux. Where the punks were once the resistance, they are now the establishment. The pirates have taken the bridge, and now they face the same conundrum all revolutionary governments face upon taking power: do you stick to your radical principles? Or do you start to make compromises, in order to keep the ship running smoothly?

The modern St. Pauli, undoubtedly, are no longer the spit-and-sawdust revolutionaries they once were. The famous skull-and-crossbones t-shirts are now sold for twenty-five euros in the club shop and have become as much of a global fashion icon as Che Guevara. Likewise, the Millerntor now contains the same array of sponsor suites and VIP boxes as any other Bundesliga stadium, as well as a working kindergarten. The club's critics often argue that they have long surrendered to the kind of bourgeois commercialism they once railed against in the fight to stop the Sport Dome project. Brux rolls his eyes at the suggestion that the club have sold out. St. Pauli were always a professional football club, he argues, and professional football is a commercial beast. Yet he admits that things have changed. The game has not only commercialised dramatically in the last thirty years, but also become vastly more mainstream, and the make-up of the St. Pauli fanbase is now very different to what it was in the 1980s. 'Back in our day, it was all very hardcore, male, working class. Now it is much more diverse. You have a lot more middle-class people, and a lot more with university degrees,' says Brux.

In part, that also reflects the changes in the Kiez itself. The neighbourhood of St. Pauli is still as raucous as ever, and the alternative left still have a huge presence in Hamburg. In 2017, protests around the G20 summit in Hamburg erupted into days of rioting and violence, which almost cost the then Hamburg mayor, a certain Olaf Scholz, his political career. Yet the Kiez has also gentrified over the years. The Hafenstraße squats have survived as a legal housing co-operative, in part because they agreed to accept lucrative development projects in the neighbouring streets. As well as the dive bars and sex shops, St. Pauli now also has its fair share of high-end restaurants and boutique fashion stores. Brux shakes his head mournfully and gives a hollow laugh when he talks about the climbing rents. 'I could have bought a house in St. Pauli for 50,000 marks back in the day, and now the young people can't even afford to rent a place in the Kiez. But that's capitalism for you. It always wins.'

In that sense, both the club and the Kiez are victims of their own success. As in so many fashionable places, there are many who fear that their popularity will end up killing what made the club and the neighbourhood special in the first place. But for all the gentrification, St. Pauli's football revolution has not yet fully devoured its own children. Even as they have grown wealthier and more successful, they have undoubtedly stayed true to many of their core principles. The club are still a leading (and sometimes lone) voice on supporters' rights, and they take their social responsibility seriously, from helping homeless people in the local neighbourhood to supporting clean water projects in developing countries. Most of all, they remain the flag-bearers of the fight against right-wing extremism in football. No professional club in the country is as vocal in its rejection of racism, sexism, homophobia and transphobia. St. Pauli are a club borne of political radicalism, and they still often act as the German game's conscience, calling out injustices and hypocrisies where others look away.

Yet not everyone can be like them. As Brux points out, the wild, revolutionary liberalism of the *Kiez* is the perfect place for a radical football club. 'You couldn't just recreate St. Pauli in some village somewhere. 'This club wouldn't work anywhere else: it's so tied up with the history of the *Kiez*, the red-light district and the left-wing scene,' he says. At other clubs – especially their larger neighbours down the road – it is a different story.

'I am that person who you find peeling St. Pauli stickers off lampposts,' says Axel Formeseyn. 'I'd be much happier if that club didn't exist at all. It still annoys me immensely that I have to share this city.'

Formeseyn is a HSV fan, and he belongs to that particular genre of football lover who seem to suffer the game more than they actually enjoy it. In his forty years following HSV, he has been a supporter, a professional critic, and even served a brief spell on the board. He has seen both the best and the worst of his chosen club, yet even now, with the wisdom of early middle-age, he still takes every defeat personally. 'I was a troubled kid growing up, a little fat boy who always had a Nutella jar under my bed. HSV were always like my best friend, and I'm still very protective of them,' he says. They were not always a good friend, he adds. 'But then I'm a person who has quite a negative psyche anyway, and from that point of view, HSV are the perfect club.'

Recent years have not been kind to HSV. In the 2010s, their endless troubles on and off the field turned a once-proud club into a running gag, a soap opera which provided ample entertainment for fans of other clubs and no end of emotional turmoil for fans like Formeseyn. Since relegation in 2018, they have faced the added injustice of repeated derby defeats to St. Pauli and several dramatic failures to win promotion back into the top flight. At times, it has felt like this is a club cursed, chronically unable to catch a break.

Yet for all the misery, they are still a footballing colossus. HSV are one of only three German teams to have ever won the European Cup, and until 2018, they were the only club who had played in every single season in Bundesliga history. They still have three times as many members as St. Pauli, making them the sixth-largest club in the country by membership. In Hamburg, their name and their badge are everywhere, as much a feature of daily life as the container ships or the herring sandwiches. 'Everyone in this city and this region has a HSV fan in their family,' says Formeseyn, who grew up just outside Hamburg in Schleswig-Holstein, the northern state which borders Denmark and links Germany to both the North Sea and the Baltic Sea. 'Aside from maybe Bayern, Schalke and Dortmund, I can't think of another club in Germany which is bigger, more charismatic, more of a cultural icon than HSV.'

HSV have always been big. They won two titles in the Weimar era, and in the 1950s, they produced one of the greatest German strikers of all time in Uwe Seeler. But it was when Formeseyn was a child that they truly became a footballing superpower. From 1977 to 1983, the club embarked on a period of dominance which few have matched before or since, winning three titles and two European trophies in the space of just six years. Two decades after the Beatles were rocking the Reeperbahn, they brought British flair back to Hamburg by signing Kevin Keegan from Liverpool, and even lured Franz Beckenbauer back out of semi-retirement in the United States. By 1983, one magazine was expressing serious concern that HSV were 'winning themselves bust', and that the relentless success would eventually lead fans to switch off. 'It really was like that. The question when I was growing up was not whether HSV had won, but whether Horst Hrubesch had scored,' says Formeseyn.

In many ways, it made sense that Hamburg should have a team of this stature. This, after all, is one of the proudest and most powerful cities in Germany. It is one of only three city states in the Federal Republic and, as the country's only gateway to the oceans, a major lynchpin of Germany's export-heavy economy. Its history as an international trade hub stretches back to the days of the Hanseatic League, or *Hansa*, the sprawling merchant network which dominated maritime trade in medieval and early modern Europe. At its height, the League's influence reached as far as London in the west to Novgorod in the east, with Hamburg at the very centre. Nowadays, around 130 million tonnes of goods still pass through Hamburg port every year,[9] and the Hansa still plays a key role in the city's identity. Car registration plates in the city all begin with 'HH' for 'Hansestadt Hamburg', and in sports journalism, Hamburg clubs are frequently referred to as 'the Hanseatics'. More than just a historical or geographical term, the word 'Hanseatic' is also part of Hamburg's self-image, shorthand for an idealised set of characteristics. On the one hand, to be Hanseatic is to be open, liberal and international in outlook. On the other hand, it is also about having reliability, integrity and razor-sharp business acumen.

'At HSV, we always want to see ourselves as Hanseatic. But for a long time, we were probably the least Hanseatic club in the world when it came to business,' jokes Formeseyn. Rather than the foresight and pragmatism of the old Hanseatic traders, the club's twenty-first-century history has instead been marked by a reckless cycle of boom and bust, which has ultimately fuelled their long-term decline.

The reasons for HSV's troubles are familiar. Like Stuttgart, their status as the biggest club in a major city is a curse as well as a blessing. Formeseyn, who spent five years on the board between 2004 and 2009, talks of the 'personal vanities and grudges' which long characterised the club's internal politics. Everyone from politicians to local billionaires wants to have their say at a club like HSV, and in a media town like Hamburg, the squabbles are often carried out in public. As well as several of the country's most influential weeklies, Hamburg is also the birthplace of Axel Springer, the group that owns Germany's all-powerful, market-leading tabloid. *Bild* is Europe's largest newspaper, the equivalent of *The Sun*, the *Daily Mail* and the *Daily Mirror* all rolled into one super-rag which can make or break political careers at will. Between the megalomania and endless media attention, there is often little room for joined-up thinking at HSV. 'We often take the best-case scenario as the starting point, instead of just focusing on continuity and stability,' says Formeseyn.

HSV are not unique in that regard. Hamburg may like to think of itself as a city of cool-headed, reliable Hanseatics, but it does occasionally have a tendency to catastrophically over-promise. One of the city's most iconic buildings is the Elbphilharmonie, a beautiful new concert hall which overlooks the harbour and has hosted everything from state visits to the draw for Euro 2024. The building was originally intended to be finished by 2010, but ended up opening a full six years later, at around eleven times the original budget. In the same year, HSV published a new set of club principles in which they declared their intention to 're-establish as one of the top five teams in the country and qualify for European competiton every year'. Two years later, they were relegated. Hamburg has never been a city short on grand visions. But in the words of former German Chancellor and proud Hamburger Helmut Schmidt: 'If you have visions, you should probably see a doctor.'

Formeseyn is one of many HSV fans who have been happy to see the club lower expectations in recent years. At a club this size, he argues, real change can never come about overnight, or even in one or two years. It is simply too big, too cumbersome for that. 'It's a bit like one of those big container ships in the port,' he says. 'You can get it to change direction, but it takes a long time and a lot of patience.'

That isn't just true in terms of squad-building and balance sheets, but also in terms of the club's whole identity. Where St. Pauli are all sharp edges and strongly held convictions, HSV are often nebulous and murky. Depending on who you ask, they can be cast as the people's club, the club of the bourgeoisie, the

'HSV are like one of those big ships': the Port of Hamburg is one of the largest in Europe, with more than 100 million tonnes of goods passing through every year. © Kit Holden

conservative club, and the club that is truly open to everyone in the city. 'The main thing is that HSV is the bigger club, and that means people can project a lot more different things onto it than they can at St. Pauli. That can be a strength and a weakness,' says Formeseyn.

As a fan of forty years, he remembers from first-hand experience when racism was commonplace on the terraces. He recalls frequent monkey noises directed at black players – even those playing for HSV – and away trips where he felt like 'the only normal person in a sea of arseholes'. Even in the modern era, when racism and far-right violence are far less common, HSV still attract many people who Formeseyn would rather not share a stadium with. 'If you're a closet Nazi in Hamburg or Schleswig-Holstein and you want to go to the football, you are obviously more likely to go to HSV than St. Pauli,' says Formeseyn. 'It was hard fighting that back in the day, and it is still hard now.'

At the same time, he is adamant that HSV's size is also a strength. Far more than St. Pauli, he says, HSV is something that can bring vastly different people together in Hamburg and provide common ground in an increasingly polarised world. 'If everyone always has to have a strong opinion on every issue, then you never get any consensus on anything. And then where does that leave you? You need to talk to each other. That's true of anything, whether it's right-wing populism, climate change, the pandemic or the speed limit. And it's also true in football,' he says.

This, arguably, is the other great tradition of German politics. In the medieval era, the Hansa constructed an entire trading empire on the basis of compromise and consensus, and in the modern era, those have also been the major strengths of post-war German democracy. Germany may have a system of proportional representation, but ever since 1949, it has been dominated by two broad-church parties: the conservative CDU and the centre-left SPD. They are known as the *Volksparteien*, or people's parties, because they both see themselves as political movements that should appeal to the broadest possible base. Angela Merkel was arguably the ultimate embodiment of this kind of politics, pushing her CDU party far into the political centre in order to sweep up as many voters as possible. She was rewarded with sixteen years in power, at the height of which almost one in two Germans were voting for her party.

Merkel's successor, Olaf Scholz, aspires to the same kind of universal appeal. As Chancellor, the former mayor of Hamburg cast himself in the role of the capable but taciturn Hanseatic, a steady hand on the tiller in times of turbulence. Yet many voters have begun to move away from parties like the CDU and the SPD, and the 2021 election was the first ever in which both parties fell below thirty per cent of the vote. German politics, once famed for its comforting predictability, has become more volatile and polarised. It is becoming harder and harder to build working majorities.

Formeseyn argues that won't change if everyone simply retreats into the comfort of tribalism. 'That's my biggest criticism of certain political parties, and it's also my biggest criticism of St. Pauli. In terms of my own values, I agree with everything St. Pauli stand for. But if all you do is sit in your corner and tell everyone else that they are doing it wrong, then where does that leave you? You don't reach the people you actually need to reach, and you'll never get a majority,' he says.

He freely admits that he doesn't have the answers. But then, that is partly his point. Grand visions and red lines are often great in theory, but they rarely work out in practice. His is an appeal for a more realistic approach to football and politics, one where things are less black and white, and colours are nailed slightly less firmly to the mast. He wants HSV to stand up for the values of tolerance and solidarity, but without telling its fans how to think. It is, perhaps, the only model for a club like HSV. It may not be quite as sexy as St. Pauli's model, but Formeseyn is willing to take that hit. 'When I was younger, I used to really want HSV to be cool like St. Pauli, but now I don't mind so much. St. Pauli is like a fashion label, it's something people choose to like. HSV is something you are born with.'

What does it mean to be a football fan? Is it a choice, or an affliction? Is it simply a form of entertainment on a Saturday afternoon, or is it also a question of politics? And if you accept that football is political, then what path do you take as a supporter? Do you choose a team that reflects your political values, as many St. Pauli fans do? Or do you try your best to advocate from within a broader church like HSV? Should there really be no football for fascists? Or is it ever OK to share a stadium with people you know to be racist, sexist or homophobic?

'That,' says Paula Scholz, 'is one of the biggest questions of my life. And to be honest, I think I still don't really know the answer.'

Scholz is a criminologist and political scientist, and a lifelong HSV fan. She meets me on the morning of derby day at the Hamburg *Fanhaus*, a red-brick early-twentieth-century detached house nestled under the train tracks in the district of Altona. The building was once a police station, but its interior is now covered with HSV stickers: it acts as both a community centre for local fan groups and as the headquarters of the *Fanprojekt*, an initiative that runs youth and education projects within the fan scene. 'For me, football was always less about the game itself and more about being part of a community,' says Scholz.

Like many football fans, she has not always had reason to be proud of that community. 'As a woman, I've experienced misogyny in the stadium, and it's always been clear that HSV fans have a reputation for being rightwing,' she says. 'Sometimes I feel like that is exactly why you should go to football. You come into contact with people you otherwise wouldn't meet, and that also gives you the chance to challenge their views. But I can also understand anyone who looks at it and says it's not for them.'

Scholz, though, is one of many people who have helped to change HSV's reputation in recent years. After joining the ultras as a teenager, she spent much of her ten years in the organised fan scene campaigning against discrimination on the terraces.

In 2022, she and others received the DFB's Julius Hirsch Award for their work with the *Netzwerk Erinnerungsarbeit* or *Netz E*, an association of fans, club employees and researchers involved in remembrance work around HSV.

Like many clubs, HSV long chose to ignore some of the darker elements of their own history. Their pre-war star striker Otto Harder – a convicted SS war criminal who oversaw thousands of deaths at a concentration camp in Hanover – was still honoured as a club hero when he died in the 1950s, with youth team players forming a guard of honour at his funeral. That has changed dramatically in recent years, to the extent that even some St. Pauli fans admit their club could take a leaf out of HSV's book. Since it was founded in 2016, Netz E has held a groundbreaking exhibition on the fan scene's role in far-right violence in the 1980s, produced workshops, city tours and podcasts on HSV's political history, and erected a memorial plaque to Nazi victims outside the stadium. In doing so, Scholz argues, they have helped the club live up to its responsibility as a public institution. 'As an organisation, HSV stand in direct continuity to everything that happened, both the crimes themselves and the way they were ignored and explained away in the years afterwards. So if we at HSV don't do this work, who will?' she says.

As with Matthias Thoma's work in Frankfurt, this is not just history for history's sake. More than just a research network, Netz E also acts as a campaign group for a more tolerant HSV, whose stated aim is also to 'highlight and counter discrimination in both the club and its fan scene.' For Scholz, that is something that goes beyond the club as an institution and into the entire sprawling community around it. 'We talk about the HSV family, but if we're a family, then ideally everybody should feel welcome. I don't think every individual HSV fan has to engage with the club's past. But I do think we should engage with issues like racism, sexism and anti-Semitism. That's our social responsibility, and as fans, the stadium is where we can change society.'

In recent years, both the club and its fans have made huge strides in tackling extremism and changing their once problematic reputation. Though there is still racism and misogyny in the stadium, the days when the club was known for far-right hooliganism are long gone. Increasingly, the fanbase are beginning to build an entirely different reputation. When Gambian HSV player Bakery Jatta was subjected to a relentless media campaign over the legitimacy of his immigration status in 2019, both the club and the fanbase were quick to rally around him, furiously condemning what many considered to be dog-whistle racism. The club's fan shop now sells merchandise with anti-racist terrace slogans, and in early 2024, the HSV Supporters Club, the club's largest official fan organisation, called on its members to take part in protests against the AfD.

'Nowadays, it is really important for HSV to show that it is against racism and open to the world. It doesn't have to be left-wing. It can be a normal, civil club, but still have clear values and be open to everyone,' says Scholz. That, she argues, is one of the benefits of football becoming more mainstream and commercialised: it puts added pressure on clubs like HSV not to simply ignore the horrors of their past or the racism in their ranks. HSV may not be a fascist-free zone like St. Pauli, but they also have a different role to play. The HSV fanbase contains the full spectrum of backgrounds and political views in Hamburg society, and that arguably makes their work against discrimination all the more important. In some ways, the clubs are an inverted image of each other. St. Pauli have become a big club on the back of the political activism of their fans. HSV have developed a political consciousness because they are such a big club.

Perhaps Germany always needs a little bit of both. This is a country built on both a broad, consensus-seeking middle-ground and a more radical revolutionary tradition. Without the strength of parties like the CDU and the SPD, Germany would arguably have never re-established itself as a peaceful democracy. But equally, without the protest movements of the 1960s, 1970s and 1980s, it would arguably be a far more conservative country, with a far less self-critical remembrance culture. Hamburg, too, would not be the football city it is with only the faded grandeur of HSV or the fashionable grit of St. Pauli. As much as Axel Formeseyn may not want to share his city, the reality is that it needs both clubs.

All that is missing now is a bit of sporting success. In years gone by, Bayern Munich president Uli Hoeness would repeatedly say that the only thing he really feared was a successful club in Hamburg. He had a point: Hamburg is bigger than Munich, wealthier than Berlin, and more international than Stuttgart or Dortmund. More than any other city in Germany, it has all the ingredients to be a football capital like Manchester or Milan and challenge the hegemony of the south. Thus far, it has not managed it. In recent decades Bavaria has reigned supreme.

MUNICH (BAVARIA)

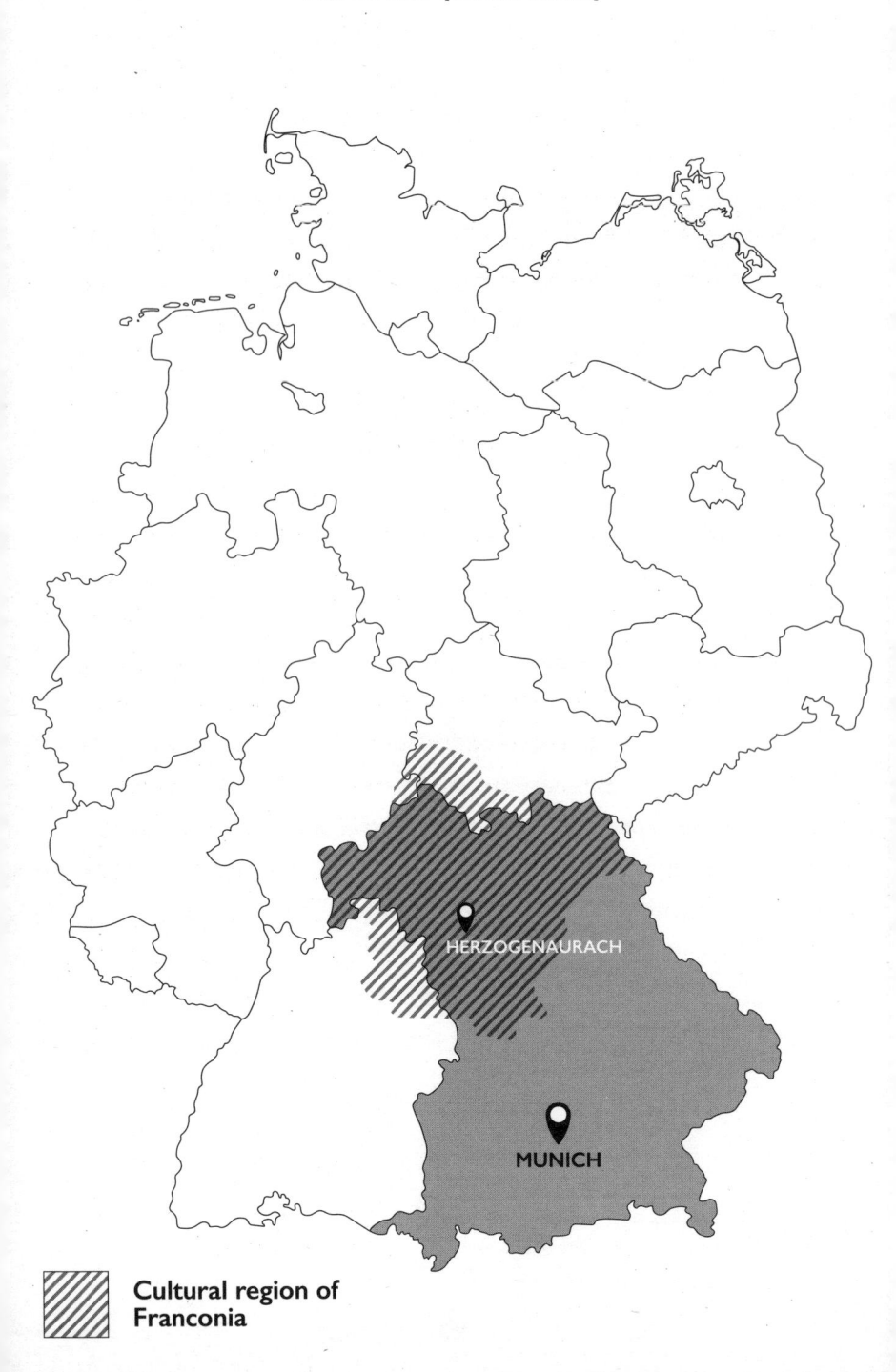

HERZOGENAURACH

MUNICH

///// **Cultural region of Franconia**

7

MUNICH
LAPTOPS AND LEDERHOSEN

Perhaps, at some point during the afternoon of 24 September 2023, Harry Kane might have wondered what he'd let himself in for. He didn't show it, of course. The Bayern Munich striker was always a consummate professional, and at thirty he knew his way around a sponsor's photo shoot as well as anyone. But as he sat there in front of an inflatable ladybird in his grey felt waistcoat and lederhosen, clutching a litre of beer in one hand and a fresh pretzel in the other, it was hard not to imagine what was going through the mind of England's captain and record goal scorer. Was that a flash of uncertainty behind the polite, pearly-white smile? A glint of fear in those friendly grey eyes?

It had been three months since Bayern had paid Tottenham Hotspur a club record €100 million fee to lure Kane to Bavaria. With seven goals in his first eight games, he was already living up to the hype. But as everyone had been telling him for weeks now, he would only really make it in Munich once he made it here. The Theresienwiese festival grounds in the city centre, home to the largest and most famous public party in the world: Oktoberfest.

The annual trip to Oktoberfest is a rite of passage for new Bayern players. Every year, the international superstars of Germany's biggest club are dolled up in traditional Bavarian dress and hauled off to the Theresienwiese to pose with beer and sausages. For the players, it is just another contractual obligation. A bite to eat, a few token swigs of Paulaner, a couple of words for the press, and they are gone. For the club as a whole, it is a hugely important branding exercise and often a barometer for the mood in the camp. In 2022, with the team in a run of bad form, Bayern's top brass looked suitably glum as they held their beers to the camera. A year later, it was all smiles after Kane had fired them to the top of the league with a hat-trick against Bochum.

Oktoberfest – or the 'Wiesn' as locals call it – is a behemoth of an event. In 2023, it attracted an estimated 7.2 million visitors, who consumed around 6.8 million litres of beer between them. The Theresienwiese itself measures around 420,000 square metres and contains thirty-eight beer tents of various sizes. For three weeks, the place is packed from ten a.m. until midnight, while beyond the grounds themselves, the festival sprawls out into the rest of Munich, consuming the city and its economy. For the sixteen days it is on, hotel prices skyrocket and the train system creaks under the weight of numbers. Everywhere you go, you see people wearing the traditional *Trachten*: lederhosen, dirndls and silly feathered hats.

The festival's origins lie in the early nineteenth century, when the citizens of Munich were invited to celebrate the marriage of Bavarian Crown Prince Ludwig to Maria Theresa. Originally, it centred around a horse race, but now all that is left of that are the elaborate horse-drawn carriages on which the major breweries parade their barrels onto the festival grounds. The only sport to be had is at the funfair, with its rollercoasters, shooting ranges and huge ferris wheel. The real business takes place in the beer tents, which are in fact enormous, temporary wooden structures, as long as a football pitch and as high as a small stadium. Inside, they can hold thousands of drinkers, many of whom stand, rather than sit on the benches. Highly skilled waiters and immensely disciplined security staff patrol the narrow aisles, bringing beer to the tables and order to the chaos. On the stage in the middle, tireless musicians thrash out a heady mix of Bavarian oompah and trashy chart hits.

It is, in other words, much as you might imagine it. Yet there are also a few key misconceptions about Oktoberfest. The first is in the name itself. In reality, the main stretch of the festival takes place in the last two weeks of September, and the whole thing is usually wrapped up by the first weekend of October. To the eternal chagrin of British tourists, there is also no such thing as a 'stein' of beer in German. At Oktoberfest, you order a *Maß*, or a litre, and the huge glass it comes in is called a *Krug*. And perhaps most importantly, Oktoberfest is not typically German. Other German cities may run their own small versions, but most self-respecting Germans would not be seen dead in lederhosen. The female figure who gazes down on the carnage from the edge of the Theresienwiese is a statue of Bavaria, not Germania. The clothes, the music and even the beer itself are also very much a regional thing. Call it what you want, but the festival is Bavarian.

Bavaria, the Germans say, is a place where the clocks tick differently. This may be the place that outsiders think of when they think of Germany, but there is no other German state that has such a distinct sense of self. In terms of food, religion and

England captain Harry Kane (left) tucks in to a *Maß* of beer alongside team mates Manuel Neuer and Jamal Musiala at Oktoberfest in 2023. © FC Bayern München

dialect, the Bavarians are often far closer to Austria than they are to much of the rest of Germany. In the Alps, they have by far the most striking landscapes in the whole country. Their traditional costumes and festivals, meanwhile, betray a conservatism which is unique among German regions. The Bavarian CSU party, which campaigns in tandem with the Christian Democrat CDU at national level, is generally seen as the more conservative wing of Germany's centre-right bloc. In Bavaria itself, it has won the largest vote share at every single post-war election, governing almost uninterrupted since 1946.

But the old Bavarian clocks also tick to a modern, global time. More than any other German region, the huge state on the Austrian and Czech border has also made itself an international brand, recognisable throughout the world. It has done so with a curious but highly successful mixture of commercialism and parochialism which is on full show at Oktoberfest. On the one hand, this is still a proud regional tradition, the highlight of the year for many people in Munich and across Bavaria. On the other hand, it is a byword for mass tourism, a mecca for Scandinavian drinkers, American families and British stag dos alike.

That particular Bavarian brew of the parochial and the global is not just a beer tent thing. Many of Germany's biggest companies, from Audi and BMW to Siemens and Allianz, were founded and are still based in Bavaria. Just like Porsche in Stuttgart, most of them began as traditional family firms from the German Mittelstand and have since become world-beating brands on the cutting edge of business, technology and manufacturing. As then German President Roman Herzog famously put it in 1998: 'In Bavaria, there is a symbiosis between laptops and lederhosen.'

That is why Harry Kane had to go to Oktoberfest. Bayern Munich may be the only German football club to have conquered the world, but just like every other major Bavarian brand, they also make a point of staying true to their roots. For many Bavarians, it is that combination which makes their unique mountain region so great. Here, they say, tradition and modernity go hand in hand, and the salt of the earth can become global market leaders. Laptops and lederhosen is the winning formula which has made Bayern a modern superclub and helped make Germany one of the leading economies in the world.

The question is: does it still work?

Bavaria is big. By land area, it accounts for roughly a fifth of modern Germany, the equivalent of around two Belgiums or a little more than half an England. And as in any big country, there is plenty of hair-splitting and nit-picking about who is really Bavarian. The state's current borders broadly reflect those of the Kingdom of Bavaria, founded in 1805. But the most Bavarian bit of Bavaria – the bit with the lederhosen, huge beers and foamy white veal sausage – is generally held to be the bit closest to the Czech and Austrian borders. This is *Altbayern*, or 'Old Bavaria', while everything else is Bavarian in name only. Culturally, most people in Nuremberg, Erlangen, Bamberg and Fürth would identify as Franconian rather than Bavarian. Likewise, those in western Bavarian cities such as Augsburg tend to see themselves more as Swabians.

'I'm from northern Bavaria, and if you ask the real Bavarians down here in Munich, they'll say that we're not really Bavarian, we're just part of the rest of Germany,' says Lothar Matthäus, Germany's World Cup winning captain from 1990. Matthäus grew up just outside Nuremberg, a city which officially and geographically lies in the heart of Bavaria. He also spent a significant chunk of his career at Bayern and now lives in Munich. Yet his accent, with its long consonants and spiky vowels, is unmistakably Franconian. Matthäus himself is less fussy about the distinction. 'I do see myself as Bavarian. Although to be honest I have spent so much time abroad that I mainly think of myself as a citizen of the world,' he shrugs.

It is true that Matthäus is an international figure. As well as a World Cup winner, he is also Germany's most capped player, an icon who has won seven German titles with Bayern, an Italian title with Inter Milan, two UEFA Cups and a Ballon d'Or. Other than Franz Beckenbauer and Gerd Müller, there are few German players who have achieved his level of global stardom, even in the modern era. 'I was lucky in that I grew up in Herzogenaurach, a town where football always played a big role,' he says. Matthäus's home town, which lies just west of Nuremberg, has fewer than 23,000 inhabitants and no train station. Yet it is home to two of the most famous and influential sports shoe producers in history: Adidas and Puma.

Bavaria has no shortage of big-name brands based in backwater towns. Cast your eye over the map of the state, and you might not recognise many of the place names, but you will recognise the companies that were born there. Fürth is the birthplace of Grundig. Ingolstadt is home to Audi. Yet few towns punch above their weight as much as Herzogenaurach. It is a town made famous, but bitterly divided, by its two iconic sneaker producers. And its story is a classic Mittelstand tale of family intrigue and infighting.

Before the Second World War, Herzogenaurach brothers Adolf and Rudolf Dassler had set up a successful business producing specialist sports shoes. Yet by the time they both returned to civilian life in Herzogenaurach in 1948, the pair had fallen out bitterly. In the wake of the feud, they set up two rival companies under their own names. 'Adi' Dassler founded 'Adidas', while 'Rudi' Dassler launched 'Ruda', which was later renamed Puma. From then on, Herzogenaurach was a small town divided, with Puma on one side and Adidas on the other. 'It was a bit like in Berlin with the Wall,' says Matthäus. 'If you went to the other side of town, you had to make sure you hid the logo on your shoes.'

Matthäus, who grew up at the height of the rivalry in the 1960s and 1970s, was in the Puma camp. Both his parents worked for Puma, his mother sewing shoes and his father as a factory caretaker. 'As a kid, I spent more time at the factory than I did at the playground,' he says. His brother still works for the company and Matthäus has now been a brand ambassador for forty-five years and counting. 'I was like Rudi Dassler's third son. We were a Puma family through and through.'

That, by extension, made him a Gladbach fan. This was the era in which Bayern and Gladbach were establishing themselves as the two major powers in German football, and that naturally attracted the attention of the country's two biggest sports brands. Adidas had been providing shoes for Bayern players since the 1960s, and in 1976, Puma became Gladbach's official supplier. In Herzogenaurach, it was not just a question of Puma or Adidas, but also of Gladbach or Bayern. 'That's why I started my career at Gladbach,' says Matthäus. 'I could have gone to trials at Bayern, but that wasn't the way I was raised.'

Ultimately, though, Matthäus had a relentless nose for success. After five years at Gladbach, he made a sensational move to Munich in 1984. 'The most difficult thing about the contract negotiations wasn't the money, it was persuading them that I had to play in Puma shoes,' he remembers. A deal was hashed out and Matthäus moved south, becoming one of the first of many major stars whom the Bavarians would poach from their rivals in the coming years. Indeed, Matthäus's transfer arguably marked the beginning of Bayern's rise to become the global superclub they are today. Though already a big name in the early 1980s, they were not yet the dominant force in German football. With HSV in their prime, Bayern hadn't won the league for three years when Matthäus arrived, and in another timeline, their best years might well have been behind them. Instead, Bayern did what no other German club has managed: they turned fleeting success into total, unrelenting hegemony.

As of 2023, Bayern have won thirty-three national championship titles in their history, more than three times as many as any other German club. Twenty-eight of those titles have come in the years since 1980, a period in which the club also won fifteen of their twenty DFB-Pokals and four of their eight European titles. Nowadays, their dominance is self-sustaining, with the steady stream of silverware bringing in ever more money and attracting ever more top players. It was Matthäus's generation that laid the groundwork, winning five titles in six years between 1985 and 1990 to kickstart an obsessive culture of winning unparalleled in modern football.

At the same time, Bayern also became a global brand, attracting both big-name sponsors and endless media attention. As football became more and more a part of mainstream pop culture in the 1990s, loud personalities like Matthäus and Stefan Effenberg plunged Bayern further into the limelight. The famous P1 nightclub on the edge of Munich's English Garden became a regular stomping ground for the club's new stars, as well as their entourage of paparazzi and gossip columnists. The club became known as 'FC Hollywood' and though the nickname may have been disparaging, Bayern thrived on the attention. 'Where's the press, where's the gossip, who is everyone talking about?' runs a line in the club's official anthem *'Stern des Südens'*, released in 1998.

Yet even in the heyday of FC Hollywood, Bayern always attempted to remain grounded. Bayern, after all, is the German word for Bavaria, and the blue and white diamonds in the club badge are taken from the traditional Bavarian flag. Whether with the Oktoberfest trips or the Christmas visits to local fan clubs, the superstars were always expected to pay due homage to the club's Bavarian roots. Matthäus remembers being asked to look after new recruits in the 1990s. 'It didn't matter if it was Andi Brehme from Bremen or Sami Kuffour from Ghana: I would take them to the beer garden and teach them about Bavarian hospitality over a beer and a pretzel,' he says.

As he sees it, that was part of Bayern's winning formula. 'At Bayern, you always felt that people were looking out for you,' he explains. 'Even when I arrived in 1984, they were asking me if I needed a car and an apartment. That was totally different to Gladbach, where I had to sort all that stuff out myself.' That kind of treatment is something Bayern players would rave about for years. They may be a big club, one which can be brutally competitive both internally and externally, but they also look after their own like few others.

Matthäus puts that down mostly to Uli Hoeness, the man who signed him for Bayern and has done more than anyone else to shape the club's success in the last four decades. Hoeness was one of the stars of Bayern's first golden generation, winning three European Cups in the 1970s before suffering a career-ending injury at the age of just twenty-seven. After taking over as general manager in 1979, he went on to define the next four decades as director, president and now honorary president. 'He took a club which was in the red financially and transformed it into a successful business,' says Matthäus. And perhaps unsurprisingly for a man who also runs his own sausage company, he ran it in the spirit of those big family firms of which Bavaria and Germany are so proud. 'On-field success is part of Bayern's DNA, but it's not everything. Uli Hoeness used to say that we can miss out on the odd title if it means retaining our identity. And that identity is the sense of family.'

That principle has also served Bayern well financially. The club may have become as slick a commercial machine as any in world football, but they have done so under their own steam. As Hoeness never tires of telling people: 'Other clubs went into the bank for a loan, Bayern went in to set up an investment account.' Even today, most clubs of Bayern's size have either an extremely wealthy owner, a mountain of debt, or both. Germany's biggest club, by contrast, have stayed true to the holy grails of conservative teutonomics: stability, steady growth and aversion to overspending. As transfer fees have skyrocketed in recent years, they have been careful not to be sucked into the arms race. Until they signed Lucas Hernandez in 2019, Bayern had never spent more than €50 million on a single player, a mark which most other superclubs had long since smashed.

That frugality doesn't necessarily make them the good guys, of course. Hoeness served two years in prison for tax evasion in 2013, and Bayern's dominance has slowly strangled the rest of the league, both in sporting and financial terms. Yet unlike the oil-rich clubs of England, France and Saudi Arabia, they can at least claim to have won a fair fight. Like any good German family firm, theirs is a success built from the ground up. Even those who hate them – which is most of the country – grudgingly admit admiration for the model.

Yet as dominant as they are, Bayern's place among the elite is also precarious. Until now, their self-made wealth has been enough to compete with the richest clubs in world football. But with ever more money pouring into the game from the Gulf and elsewhere, even Bayern have had to reassess some of their scruples. 'There was once a time when Hoeness said there would never be a €100 million transfer, and now they have paid that for Kane,' says Matthäus. 'I hope Bayern can stay true to their values and keep their feet on the ground, but they also need to adapt and find new ways to be successful.'

If they ever need a reminder of how far you can fall, Bayern don't need to travel to Manchester, Milan or any of the other fallen giants of world football. All they need to do is go a few kilometres across town.

'Bayern do the laptops and lederhosen thing. We are sort of the alternative. We're not as obsessed with winning, and we're not as commercialised as them,' says Stephanie Dilba. 'Although if we're completely honest, that has less to do with idealism, and more to do with incompetence.'

Dilba is a fan of TSV 1860 Munich, the other grand old club in the city. Though as she sees it, it is Bayern who are 'the other club'. Nicknamed 'the Lions' in honour of Bavaria's national animal, 1860 are as proud a club as their city rivals, and they tend to describe themselves as 'Munich's great love'. Until the 1960s, they really did have a claim to be the biggest team in the Bavarian capital. Even as Bayern boomed in the latter half of the twentieth century, 1860 always harboured hopes of matching their neighbour's meteoric success. But where Bayern got everything right, 1860 seemed to get everything wrong. In the last thirty years, they have been repeatedly chewed up and spat out by the machine of modern football. They are now stuck, somewhat traumatised, in the third division.

As their name suggests, 1860 are a club with a long history, and Dilba knows it better than most. A teacher by trade, she has been a Lions fan since the 1980s and has seen the club from all angles. She has worked in the youth system, campaigned against racism on the terraces, and written one of the seminal books on the club's history. She still lives a stone's throw from the Grünwalder Stadion, where 1860 play their home games, and has spent years running walking tours around the area. 'Giesing is traditionally a worker's district,' she says, as we walk past the residential buildings of the neighbourhood in southern Munich. 'This is where the normal people live.'

This is the classic distinction that people make between Bayern and 1860. Bayern are the affluent, middle-class club from bourgeois Schwabing in the north, whose fans are glory hunters from anywhere and everywhere. 1860 are the authentic Munich club from working-class Giesing. 'If you're really from Munich, you're a Lion,' says the slogan on Dilba's t-shirt. While many would take issue with that idea, the two clubs are undoubtedly chalk and cheese. Even the most die-hard Bayern fan would admit that their home games are more of a commercial event. At 1860, things are decidedly more down to earth.

When I meet Dilba near the stadium on matchday, the streets are packed, with a sell-out crowd of 15,000 expected for a third-tier game. For pre-game beers, some of the fans gravitate towards an open-air community project on the corner of an intersection, while others head to the local skatepark, where the ultras are selling t-shirts and bottled beers. As we walk around, almost every second person seems to greet Dilba like a long-lost cousin. This is a community club, with deep roots in both Giesing and the wider region. On the winding road up to the stadium, fans from across Bavaria are arriving on specially arranged coaches. Some of them have set up makeshift food stalls, where they sell Bavarian specialties like *Leberkäs*, a kind of spongy pink meatloaf, from tupperwares and tin foil. 'A lot of them come from the countryside, so they'll bring their own produce,' says Dilba. This is a long way from Oktoberfest. There is not a laptop in sight.

Yet as Dilba points out, the Munich rivalry is more complicated than just big versus small. 1860 got their name from the year they were founded, and at that time, football was still unheard of in Germany. The 'TSV' stands for 'Turn- und Sportverein', and the club's original focus was on 'Turnen', the form of German gymnastics that boomed on the back of nineteenth-century nationalism. By the mid-1800s, the Turnen movement had become a major part of the liberal and democratic movements which were fomenting revolution in Germany and was the sport of choice among an increasingly influential middle class. '1860 were a typical club for Turnen, and that meant they were founded by the moneyed bourgeoisie,' says Dilba. It was only in 1899 that the club added a football section, and later still that the footballers moved to Giesing and began to establish their reputation as a team for the working class.

Even then, 1860's establishment clout continued well into the Nazi era and beyond. Nowadays, the received wisdom in German football is that 1860 were the team closest to the Nazi regime, while Bayern were maligned as a Jewish club. That is too simplistic, and some have argued that Bayern have tended to overlook their own complicity in the regime. Yet it is true that Bayern had more active Jewish members, and that they arguably faced a more dramatic caesura than 1860 when the Nazis came to power. As Dilba points out, 1860's hierarchy maintained strong relationships with the Nazi authorities and sold their stadium to the city of Munich for a favourable price after hitting financial trouble in the 1930s. Bayern's Jewish president, Kurt Landauer, by contrast, was forced to flee the country in 1938 after a brief internment in Dachau.

The Giesing club arguably remained top dogs until the 1960s, when they celebrated both their centenary and their footballing golden era. It was 1860, not Bayern, who joined the Bundesliga as a founding member in 1963. In the following three years, they won the cup, reached the European Cup Winners' Cup final against West Ham, and eventually became league champions in 1966. Their fans still sing about that title, and on some level, it is still the yardstick by which 1860 measure themselves. That, in turn, is the enduring paradox of the club's identity. Though proud to be the smaller, authentic club from the working-class district, they also have a sense of themselves as the city's real football grandees. 'That is also a typical 1860 trait. We have these delusions of grandeur, and we think of ourselves as being much bigger than we are because of our history,' says Dilba. More often than not, that has led to disaster.

Nowhere is that more tangible than at the Grünwalder Stadion. One of the most iconic grounds of German football history, the stadium in Giesing is also a relic. With its dystopian 1980s fencing and uncovered terraces, it is not even fit to host second-division games, and you would scarcely believe that it once drew crowds of 35,000. When 1860 initially had it built in the 1920s, it was the largest stadium in southern Germany. The project ultimately bankrupted them, and they were forced to sell the stadium to the city in 1937. It has been in public hands ever since, which in turn has become something of a neurosis for the club and its fans.

For starters, it has meant an ongoing squabble about whose home it really is. Bayern started renting the stadium from 1860 in 1925, and the two clubs continued to share it until the early 1970s. The Bayern reserves still play there, and their fans mockingly refer to it as the 'Hermann-Gerland-Kampfbahn', in reference to their long-time reserve team coach. Dilba, though, insists that it belongs in spirit to 1860 and nobody else. 'Ask anyone what this stadium is called, and they will say it's the Sechz'ger Stadion,' she huffs. 'It's our home, it's where we won the league, it's part of our identity.' But even 1860 have not played there continuously, and the club has spent much of the last half century in exile from their spiritual home.

When Munich hosted the Olympics in 1972, both Bayern and 1860 moved across town into the new, futuristic Olympiastadion. While the huge arena was a welcome new home for upwardly mobile Bayern, all it gave to 1860 was a sense of having lost a part of their identity. 'Initially, there were bigger crowds in the Olympiastadion, but we tended to win more in the old stadium, and when we started losing, the crowds dwindled too,' says Dilba. By the early 1980s, the club had hit rock bottom in the third tier and returned to the Grünwalder with their tails between their legs.

The years that followed were some of the darkest from a football perspective, but Dilba remembers them as a golden age. It was here, with the club battling to get out of the regional leagues, that she first became a fan. She recalls a sense of community, and a feeling that the club was rooted in Giesing. 'When we missed out on promotion in 1990, I saw grown men crying at the final whistle,' she says. 'Football was more emotional then. The money has changed that, I think.'

When 1860 did go up, the money started pouring in again. The club returned to the Bundesliga in 1994, and soon started to make big plans for a bright future. Buoyed by on-field success and exploding interest, president Karl-Heinz Wildmoser scrapped plans to redevelop the Grünwalder Stadion, instead moving back into the Olympiastadion and agreeing a deal with Bayern to jointly fund the construction of a new stadium for the 2006 World Cup. 1860 were now back in the big time, with dreams of becoming an equal partner to their world-beating neighbours. '1860 fans always thought that we really belonged among the elite, and suddenly you had this president who was saying that he was going to take us back there and make us the new FC Bayern,' says Dilba ruefully.

If anything, though, the new stadium turned out to be even worse for 1860 than the Olympiastadion. The Allianz Arena, which sits on the edge of the motorway in the far north of Munich, is the polar opposite of the Grünwalder Stadion. It looks like a spaceship, and to get there on public transport, you have to walk across almost a kilometre of barren, concrete concourse, which Dilba describes as a 'moonscape'. Both geographically and spiritually, it is hard to imagine a part of the city that is further from the 'normal people' in Giesing.

Back home: 1860 Munich fans have now returned to their spiritual home in front of the iconic 1950s-era scoreboard at the Grünwalder (or 'Sechz'ger') Stadion. © Matthias Koch

Worst of all, history repeated itself. Despite some early success, 1860 once again failed to live up to the size and glamour of their new stadium. As the results turned bad, crowds dwindled to nothing. The older fans preferred to watch the reserves in the Grünwalder, while the casual fans disappeared entirely. Eventually, the club's financial situation became so dire that they had to sell their shares in the stadium to Bayern. A few years later, still facing bankruptcy, they were forced to do what all German fans fear most and sell a chunk of their club to an outside investor. Since 2011, 1860 has only been forty per cent member-owned, with the other sixty per cent belonging to the Jordanian entrepreneur Hassan Ismaik.

'That time was horrible. We were going nowhere in sporting terms, were paying rent to play in a stadium we hated, and suddenly the club didn't even belong to us anymore. It got worse and worse, ever more desolate,' says Dilba. When 1860 were relegated from the second division in 2017 and then failed to obtain a licence even for the third division, she was one of many who were secretly relieved. The financial hit of going down into the fourth tier meant that the club had to cancel their rental contract at the Allianz Arena and moved back into the Grünwalder Stadion. For the first time in twenty-two years, 1860 were back in their spiritual home. 'That first game back was honestly so wonderful. I remember walking through Giesing and just seeing happy, smiling faces on every corner. Even the McDonalds had balloons outside with the words "Welcome back".'

1860 remain a deeply divided club. Ismaik, who is still majority owner, is hugely controversial. Since he saved 1860 from bankruptcy back in 2011, the Jordanian has failed to deliver on his promise of a bright new future, launched repeated attacks on both the media and the fans, and even mounted a legal challenge against the 50+1 rule. These days, the ultras regularly hold up banners that show his face crossed out. For many in Germany, 1860 are now the ultimate warning against selling out, the living proof that big spending and wealthy investors often bring more trouble than success.

Yet against that backdrop, the club's return to the Grünwalder Stadion offers some hope for fans like Dilba. 1860's attempts to keep up with Bayern ultimately drove the club into ruin, but it also made many people see what they really wanted from football. 'If you ask me where I would like to be in ten years, the main thing would be to get rid of this investor. Other than that, I just want to be here in Giesing,' she says. 'Success is great, don't get me wrong. But professional football is such a dirty business these days that it's not really any fun. I'm quite happy in the third division.'

Even at Bayern, the serial winners who consider themselves European royalty, there are those who yearn for the quiet life. In recent decades German football has carved out a niche for itself where it can have the best of both worlds: high-quality football in a top-five European league, and a fan-friendly culture which prioritises local supporters over lucrative global markets. But it is an uneasy balance. It is becoming harder and harder for German clubs to keep pace with the biggest spenders in world football. And the more the Bundesliga strains to stay afloat, the further it drifts away from the ideals of most German football fans.

'The first time I ever saw Bayern on TV, they lost 3–1 to Borussia Mönchengladbach. I think I instinctively sympathised with the losers,' says Alexander Salzweger with a wry smile.

Several decades on, in autumn 2023, the notion that you could become a Bayern fan out of sympathy seems absurd. The club have just won their eleventh league title in a row, and are fresh from a thumping, but entirely predictable, 7–0 win over Bochum. Salzweger sighs. 'Sometimes I think it would be really nice if someone else won the title for once. Or even better, for us to not qualify for the Champions League.'

Salzweger is the spokesperson for Club Nr. 12, a fan organisation which was founded in the 1990s to organise the tifos on Bayern's famous *Südkurve*. Though not officially part of the ultras, it overlaps with several of Bayern's groups and often acts as a mouthpiece for the organised fan scene, both externally and internally. This is a side of Bayern which is very different to the gaudy glitz and glamour of the Allianz Arena. The Club Nr. 12's headquarters are hidden away on the first floor of an unassuming mid-century building squeezed between a concert venue, a parcel depot and the S-Bahn train tracks just west of Munich city centre. Above the sofa in the corner, there is a huge three-dimensional cardboard model of Bayern's original emblem, a handful of commemorative pendants, and a framed picture of 'Trompeter Manni', a trumpet-playing legend of the Munich fan scene. Just opposite, there is a small bar, which is covered in stickers. Salzweger is not drinking today. 'I was at the Wiesn yesterday,' he explains, with a hungover grimace.

For such a huge club, Bayern have always had a remarkably vibrant organised fan scene. The ultras tend to maintain good relations with the club hierarchy, an arrangement that keeps ticket prices low and gives fans a voice – or at the very least a privileged ear – in many of the big decisions. 'I wouldn't say we never argue with the board, but generally it's give and take, and they give us a lot as well,' says Salzweger. It is also one of Germany's more progressive fan scenes, which Salzweger puts down to the general feeling in Munich. Bavaria may be deeply conservative, but Munich tends to vote Green and Social Democrat. As well as campaigning against racism and homophobia, the ultra group Schickeria have also been at the heart of efforts to honour Bayern's pioneering Jewish pre-war president Kurt Landauer.

The ultras' main job, though, is to keep the stadium noisy. Opposing fans often sneer at the muted atmosphere in the Allianz Arena, and even Salzweger admits that it is one of the quieter grounds in Germany. 'During Oktoberfest, we are just happy if people can even stand up straight and hold on to their beers,' he jokes, but there are also other challenges. As the biggest club in Germany, Bayern attract fans from across the country and beyond, and on any given day, the crowd contains a large proportion of tourists, day-trippers and families who tend not to make quite as much noise as hardcore fans. 'It's the classic problem of a big club which is too successful,' says Salzweger.

It is not just in terms of atmosphere that Bayern tend to struggle with their own success. Until Leverkusen's title win in 2024, the Munich giants' dominance of domestic competition was becoming toxic even to their own brand. As Germany's leading club, Bayern have a vested interest in both a strong Bundesliga and their own success in European competition. In recent years, those two goals have clashed. As they scramble to stay competitive with clubs like Manchester City and Real Madrid, Bayern's own wealth and willingness to spend have steadily increased, widening the gap between them and the rest of the Bundesliga. In the 2000s, Bayern's ups and downs meant that German football went twelve years without a European title, but the Bundesliga produced five different champions in the space of a decade. Between 2010 and 2020, Bayern brought two Champions League titles back to Germany but suffocated their domestic competition. The club can now pump so much money into their squad that even their worst teams are usually better than the rest. 'There have been a few years where we have played terrible football, and it's still enough to win the league,' grumbles Salzweger. 'That's a problem.'

It is a problem because, for all their dominance, trashing the rest of the league beyond repair is not actually Bayern's vibe. After all, the laptops and lederhosen philosophy is partly about protecting those around you. Just as Germany's major manufacturing giants rely on regional small and medium-sized businesses to provide them with materials and services, Bayern need healthy domestic rivals to keep them competitive and maintain a reliable pool of affordable talent. Under Uli Hoeness, Bayern made a point of helping out cash-strapped rivals. In the early 2000s, they organised fundraiser friendlies for clubs like St. Pauli and Union Berlin, and even loaned Borussia Dortmund €2 million to stave off bankruptcy in 2004. They also maintained a strong core of German players in their squads, and tended to take German firms like Telekom, Opel, Audi and Adidas as major sponsors. 'As the market leader in German football, Bayern always wanted to partner with the biggest German firms, even if they could get more money elsewhere,' says Salzweger. That was always part of the club's self-image, he adds: a superclub, yes, but one that did things the German way, and stayed true to its roots.

Perhaps the best example of that came in Bayern's reaction to the failed Super League project in 2021. When Europe's elite clubs launched a controversial bid to break away from European football's traditional structures and form their own franchise, it took huge fan protests in London and Manchester to persuade the English clubs involved to back down and torpedo the project. Bayern and Dortmund, by contrast, didn't even dare sign up in the first place. 'Our members and fans are against a Super League,' said Bayern president Herbert Hainer when he outlined the club's position two days after the project was announced. In Germany, there was an instinctive understanding that fans would never accept a competition that took traditional clubs out of domestic competition and put them in a new global franchise. 'The Bayern directors understood better than most of the others what was at stake, and that was good to see,' says Salzweger.

Yet there have been other battles. In 2018, Bayern agreed a sleeve sponsorship deal with Qatar Airways, a decision which prompted widespread outrage among fans. Some pointed to the human rights abuses which had been exposed in Qatar in the build-up to the 2022 World Cup. Others were queasy about Bayern, a club with a proud Jewish history, endorsing a state that is known for having strong ties to Hamas. Most of all, though, the decision to suddenly sign a Qatari airline as a major sponsor seemed to undermine Bayern's claim to be the good guys. Barcelona and Paris Saint-Germain may take Qatari money, the argument went, but Bayern were above that. 'That was what made the debate so emotional. People were saying that we shouldn't stoop to this level, we shouldn't throw everything away for a few euros more,' says Salzweger.

In the end, fan power won out once again. After years of protests on the Südkurve and one particularly acrimonious AGM, Bayern eventually cut their ties with Qatar Airways in 2023. Yet ultimately, both the Super League and the sponsorship squabble were only temporary victories. The club's argument in the Qatar debate was always that they needed that kind of lucrative sponsorship deal to remain competitive internationally. And as Salzweger admits, that is a reality which will not change any time soon. 'We can ask the question whether it's right to spend €100 million euros plus all the agents' fees on a thirty-year-old player like Harry Kane, but in the end, Bayern have to play the game if they want to compete for the Champions League.'

The only real solution, he argues, would be to have Europe-wide regulation in the form of spending and salary caps, which would level the playing field and give less wealthy clubs a chance to be more competitive. That is something that fans and Bayern directors have been arguing for more and more in recent years, but to little avail. 'It just isn't in the interest of the rich clubs and their owners,' says Salzweger. 'And as long as that's the case, it isn't going to happen. Football governance wouldn't be the first area in which Germany earnestly did things its own way, only to be disappointed that the rest of Europe had no interest in following suit.

Until now, at least, Bayern's compromise between soul and success has allowed them to take the best of modern football's wealth and mostly reject the very worst. Increasingly, though, it is leaving them stranded between ever weaker competition at home and ever stronger competition abroad. That presents them with a difficult choice. Do they go all out to stay in the European elite, leaving the Bundesliga and their roots behind entirely? Or do they rein themselves in, and risk losing their ability to compete with the very best?

That is also a question which the Bundesliga as a whole is struggling with. There is a general consensus that Bayern's dominance makes the league less appealing, but little agreement on how to solve the issue. Some, including Bayern's honorary president Uli Hoeness, see the 50+1 rule as the problem. Abolishing the regulation, they argue, would make the league more attractive to outside investors and boost its competitiveness. Fan groups and traditionalists tend to take the opposing view. They point to clubs like 1860 as proof that investors don't guarantee success and say that 50+1 protects the unique fan culture which is currently the Bundesliga's greatest asset.

In the end, it is a similar conundrum to the one facing Germany's economy. Just as the automobile giants have had to adapt to new competition in China and the USA, so too Germany's football behemoth must keep the pace with the new money in England, Saudi Arabia and Qatar. Just as major shipping cities like Hamburg and Duisburg are weighing up the dangers and opportunities of Chinese investment, so too the Bundesliga must find its own compromise between its core values and its economic interests.

Laptops and lederhosen may yet prove to be a winning formula for years to come. But even the name itself suggests that it is due an overhaul. In 1998, the laptop was the most high-tech thing a German President could possibly imagine. In 2023, even the most entrenched Bavarian conservative is probably on TikTok. It is not just football that is changing fast, but the whole world. And as the foundations of the old world continue to shake, Germany is still trying to find its place in the new one.

But if there is one place in Germany that knows better than anywhere else how to survive epochal change, it is Berlin.

BERLIN, 1945–1990

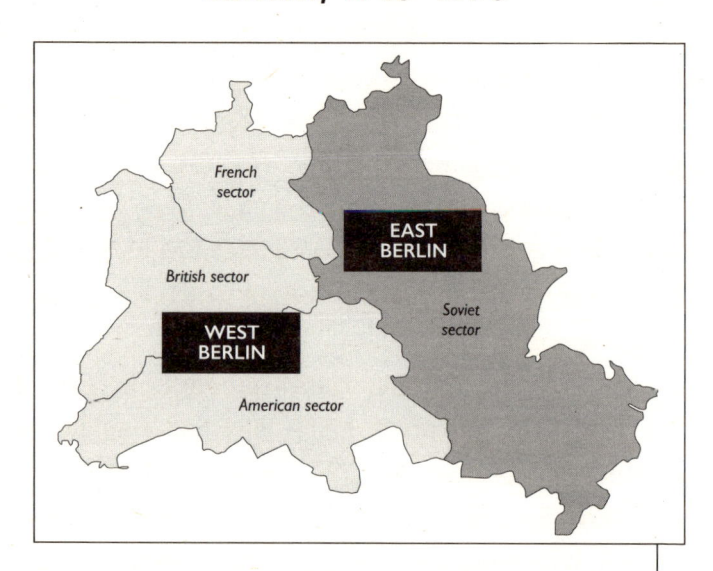

- French sector
- British sector
- American sector
- Soviet sector
- WEST BERLIN
- EAST BERLIN

DIVIDED GERMANY, 1945–1990

- BERLIN
- WEST GERMANY
- EAST GERMANY

8
BERLIN
TURNING POINT

In February 2022, Olaf Scholz stepped up to the lectern in the Bundestag in Berlin and addressed the MPs in front of him. He had done so countless times before: as a member of parliament, as finance minister under Angela Merkel, and now as German Chancellor. But this time, the stakes were higher. The speech he was about to give would immediately go down as one of the most important in German political history. Vladimir Putin's Russia had just launched a full-scale invasion of Ukraine, war had returned to the European continent, and Germany was going to have to change. The whole of Europe, said Scholz, was going through a *Zeitenwende*.

It was a big word. Zeitenwende literally means 'time-turn', and in English it is usually translated as 'turning point' or 'change of eras'. Since 2022, it has become synonymous with a similarly seismic change in geopolitics. Scholz, often characterised as the kind of dull, emotionless technocrat who could make even decisions of life and death seem boring, was pulling no punches this time. 'Zeitenwende means that we now live in a different world,' he said.

The Russian invasion of Ukraine did change Germany. Scholz's speech ushered in a huge rise in military spending, which ended decades of post-war pacifism. Western sanctions against Putin's regime also exposed Germany's reliance on Russian gas, prompting a major rethink of energy policy. That not only hit an economy that was already reeling from the Covid pandemic, but also deepened existing political divides over climate change, trade and immigration. When the Society of the German Language declared 'Zeitenwende' to be their official word of the year the following winter, they noted that 'many people experienced an emotional shift, amid new fears of nuclear conflict and a Third World War'. In the thirty years since reunification, Germans had grown used to the idea of peace, prosperity and progress. Now, they were waking up to a new world – and a new Germany.

Nowhere was that more obvious than in the capital. Berlin is the closest major western city to Ukraine, lying just fifty miles from the Polish border and only a day's drive from Lviv. It is a city that knows the horrors of war all too well and was once itself on the front line of tensions between Moscow and the West. Perhaps most importantly of all, it is a city that can recognise a momentous change when it sees it.

Change has been the only constant in the history of Berlin. The city lies on a flat, unprotected plain in the heart of Europe, which has historically made it especially susceptible to dramatic, violent transformations. In 1806, Napoleon swept through the Brandenburg Gate and declared a new European order. The revolution of 1918–19, which pushed the Kaiser off his throne and established the Weimar Republic, was ultimately decided on the streets of Berlin. In the 1930s, the Nazis planned to transform the city into a grotesquely oversized 'world capital', complete with a 300-metre-high domed hall and a 100-metre-tall triumphal arch. Instead, Hitler's warmongering reduced Berlin to rubble, and left it physically divided for nearly half a century. In 1989, the fall of the Berlin Wall heralded the end of the Cold War and the beginning of a new era of peace in Europe.

The relentless change means that Berlin does not exude old power like other European capitals do. Vienna has its great palaces and concert houses; Berlin's most famous cultural institutions are modernist theatres and fetish clubs. London and Paris are the economic lifeblood of the UK and France; Berlin has a lower GDP per capita than most other major German cities.[10] Berlin is ramshackle, it has no natural centre, and it certainly doesn't have airs and graces. Its most famous dish is currywurst, a tasteless sausage slathered in ketchup and curry powder which was invented at a time of post-war food shortages and is usually inhaled standing up. Berlin does not sit down. It is a place where nothing lasts, and everything is built on sand, where radical ideas are tested and revolutions rise and fall.

Berlin football has always been shaped by its history. The city's clubs, its derbies, its fan culture and its stadiums are all intimately tied to the sweeping geopolitical dramas that have forged it over the last hundred years. The capital's biggest football ground, the Olympiastadion, is a lasting relic of the Nazis' architectural megalomania, complete with grotesque, muscular statues, mounted iron torches and vast, sweeping stone plazas. Its two major clubs, Hertha BSC and 1. FC Union, emerged on either side of the Berlin Wall, and their respective histories tell mirror-image stories of a divided city.

But now, both the city and its football are changing once again. For the last three decades, Berlin has enjoyed more stability than it ever had in the century before. But peace and prosperity have also brought new problems. In recent years, the influx of investment has brought new wealth and opportunities to Berlin, but also pushed up rents, gentrified iconic neighbourhoods, and plunged the city into a chronic housing crisis. That in turn has eaten away at the capital's world-famous cultural scene and left it bitterly divided over its own future.

Those changes are also playing out on the field. For much of the post-war era, Berlin's clubs had gotten used to lagging behind those in other major cities. But now, the city's newfound prosperity is also breathing new life into its football. New powers are rising and new revolutions are taking shape. In Berlin, perhaps more than anywhere else, the game reflects a country in flux.

For a few moments on the evening of 12 December 2023, the Olympiastadion turned upside down. It was a little before ten p.m., Luka Modric had just missed a penalty for Real Madrid, and the half-time whistle was only seconds away. Union Berlin's goalkeeper, Frederik Rønnow, pumped a long ball upfield, happy enough just to get to the break with the score at 0–0. The ball bounced awkwardly for the Madrid back line, and suddenly, miraculously, there was an opening. Kevin Volland scampered into it like a dog with a stolen pork chop and nudged the ball past Kepa Arrizabalaga. There was a split second of silence as it bobbled over the line, and then: an explosion. The Olympiastadion, with its foundations of 1930s concrete and its modern fibreglass roof, seemed to tremble under the noise.

In truth, the old stadium had seen bigger earthquakes than this. This was where Jesse Owens stuck it to Hitler at the 1936 Olympics and where Usain Bolt broke the 100m world record in 2009. It was where Zinedine Zidane landed his infamous headbutt on Marco Materazzi's chest in the 2006 World Cup final and where Lionel Messi won his last ever Champions League title with Barcelona in 2015. Yet for the Union fans at least, all of that was barely a tremor in comparison to Volland's toe-poked finish in 2023. For them, this was bigger. Much, much bigger.

Little more than a decade earlier, Union had been in the third division, a club with little glamour and even less money. Their beloved Alte Försterei stadium – a crumbling, GDR throwback out in the woods of south-eastern Köpenick – had been on the verge of abandonment, and the club itself had only just avoided bankruptcy a few years earlier. Now, they were here: 1–0 up against Real Madrid in front of a sell-out crowd of 75,000 Berliners. In little over a decade, Union had written one of the greatest fairytales of the modern European game. And in doing so, they had also transformed Berlin football.

Berlin, famously, is not a football city. As of 2023, it has just two fully professional teams. Union, the cult club from the former East, have only been in the Bundesliga since 2019. A yo-yo team in the GDR, they almost disappeared entirely after the Wall came down, surviving only thanks to the fierce loyalty of their own fans. Their western neighbours, Hertha, are traditionally the much bigger club, and have long harboured dreams of joining German football's elite. Yet they struggle to fill the vast Olympiastadion and have spent most of their recent history veering between crisis and mediocrity. Both clubs command only limited support outside their core neighbourhoods, and the last time either of them won a major trophy was in 1968. As one old Berlin souvenir shop joke has it: 'We can do everything in this city – except football.'

On first glance at least, this is odd. Other European capitals all have their major clubs: Madrid have all-powerful Real and eleven-time champions Atlético. In Rome, SS Lazio and AS Roma have five Scudettos and sixteen Coppa Italia wins between them. In London, Arsenal, Chelsea and Tottenham can boast twenty-one league titles, while West Ham, Crystal Palace and Fulham are also regular fixtures in the top flight. Until the Second World War, Berlin was cut from much the same cloth. Between 1903 and 1931, three of its clubs were crowned German champions, with another three making the championship final. But then came the Nazis, the Second World War, and perhaps most importantly, the Wall.

After the defeat of Nazi Germany in 1945, Berlin was divided first into four zones of occupation, and later between the two German states. The divided city was the heart of the new Cold War, the place where two competing systems rubbed up against each other and tensions inevitably flared. In 1948, the Soviets blockaded West Berlin in an ultimately unsuccessful bid to bring it under their own sphere of influence. Thirteen years later, the two halves of the city were sealed off from one another when the GDR built a wall to stop its own citizens from leaving. And in football as in everything else, that put Berlin on a different path. 'The Wall stunted Berlin's development as a global city,' says Union fan Olaf Forner. 'We weren't able to develop in the same way as other major capitals.'

Forner is an institution of the Union fan scene, and he knows Berlin inside out. For the last twenty-five years, he has worked as a news vendor, one of a dying breed who roam the city's cafés and bars in the evenings. Like Berlin, he is also one of a kind: immediately recognisable by his straggly long blond hair, his beaming smile, and the bright red Union shirt pulled tightly over his proud-father-of-two belly. And like Berlin, he is also a shape-shifter. At night, he is the *Taz-Unioner*, the Union fan who sells the *Taz* newspaper to the capital's many avid drinkers. In his day job, he works for a charity which supports people with disabilities. At weekends, he works for Union, selling programmes, spare tickets, books and artworks in and around the stadium.

Now in his mid-fifties, Forner was born just a few years after the Wall went up, and he is very much a product of divided Berlin. He grew up in Mahlsdorf, on the very eastern fringes of East Berlin, but had regular contact with his extended family in the West. Though they had decided to stay in the GDR to avoid losing their property, his parents were religious, and they had little love for the strictly atheist communist state. Forner remembers living a kind of double life in his childhood: at school, there was only the party line, while at home, he received a far more critical education. 'We rarely watched East German TV at home, and it was always clear that we should always be careful of what we said outside of the house. I grew up living in two separate worlds, like a kind of schizophrenia,' he says.

That was true of football too. Nowadays, Hertha and Union are arch-rivals, but Forner grew up supporting both clubs. At weekends, he would go to watch Union, who despite their lack of on-field success were still the most popular club in East Berlin. Yet he also had family ties to Hertha, his grandfather having grown up just a short distance from their former stomping ground in northern Berlin. Though he couldn't cross the border to see them live, Forner followed the West Berlin club avidly via western TV and the magazines his grandmother sent him from the other side of the Wall. 'I supported Union in the stadium and Hertha through the media,' he says.

As he points out, that wasn't unusual. Most East German football fans also had a favourite West German team, and in Berlin, Hertha and Union fans had developed strong ties from the 1970s onwards. Union fans would travel to see Hertha if they played against Eastern European opposition, while Hertha fans would occasionally make the trip across the border to watch Union games. Forner was one of many fans who wore a badge on his jacket with the emblems of both clubs and the words 'Friends behind barbed wire'. 'There was an anti-GDR, anti-state element to it which appealed to a lot of us,' he says. Hertha, after all, were a club from the capitalist-imperialist West, and the East German authorities frowned upon any fraternisation with the class enemy. Together, the two fanbases would also poke fun at BFC Dynamo, the Stasi-backed East Berlin club who dominated GDR football for much of the 1980s. As BFC stormed to ten East German titles in a row, making them the most successful club in Berlin football history, Hertha and Union fans insisted there were 'only two champions on the Spree: Union and Hertha BSC!'

The joke, of course, was that neither club had any hope of being champions. In East Berlin, Union were kept small by a system which funnelled the best players and best facilities towards BFC. Though they often drew the larger crowds, they never had any chance of catching their rivals, and spent most of the 1970s and 1980s yo-yoing between the first and second divisions. Meanwhile, in the freedom of the West, Hertha faced their own problems. West Berlin, at that time, was completely surrounded by communist GDR. It was an island city on the frontline of the Cold War, which had been blockaded once before in 1949 and still operated under slightly different rules to the rest of West Germany. Residents of West Berlin were exempt from military service, for example, which made it attractive for artists and creatives looking to dodge the draft. For footballers, the prospect of playing in a besieged city was less enticing. While cities like Hamburg, Munich and Cologne could easily attract the best players, clubs in West Berlin had to get creative. In the mid-1960s, Hertha were kicked out of the Bundesliga for paying illegal bonuses. And for most of the forty-year division, neither Hertha nor Union had much to shout about.

When the Wall came down, there was hope of a new beginning on both sides. In January 1990, the two teams played a highly symbolic friendly match at the Olympiastadion, at which the two sets of fans mingled happily in the stands and basked in the afterglow of the fall of the Wall two months earlier. In their match report the following day, *Der Tagesspiegel* newspaper declared there were 'no losers, only winners', but in reality, both clubs lost out in the years after reunification. Hertha were relegated in 1991, while Union, like many other eastern clubs, struggled to make the transition to capitalism and descended into a period of chaos and decline. Rather than football, most Berliners threw themselves into a period of wild cultural experimentation, as techno clubs, squats and artists' collectives sprung up like daisies in the derelict buildings of East Berlin. 'Berlin had so much else to offer: parties, social projects, art, everything,' says Forner, who also drifted away from football in the early 1990s. 'It's not like Gelsenkirchen or Dortmund, where football is all they have. Here, football is just a side note.'

It was also, crucially, a fragmented city. The Wall had not only stunted the development of clubs like Hertha and Union, but it had also mangled the city's topography. The scars of the division had left Berlin with no natural centre, no common economic and social history. More than any other big European city, it had become a loose collection of individual boroughs, each with their own history and their own identity. The football landscape reflected that, with most clubs appealing to a specific local niche. Multicultural Kreuzberg had Türkiyemspor, the team founded by Turkish immigrants to West Berlin in the 1970s. Eastern Hohenschönhausen was home to the Stasi's most notorious prison, and the GDR's one-time Stasi-backed giants BFC Dynamo. Affluent Charlottenburg had Tennis Borussia, the club of the western intellectuals.

Hertha were the only club who even attempted to unite the whole city under one banner. Their pre-war titles and their more recent fan friendship with Union meant they were the one team that had support in both the former East and the former West, and when they reached the Champions League in 1999, it seemed plausible that they might become a major power in reunified Germany. But in reality, Hertha were always too thinly spread, their stadium too large and too far out of town to become Berlin's equivalent of Bayern or HSV. After their brief foray into the big time, they quickly returned to mid-table mediocrity, and for the next twenty years, became trapped in a cycle of huge dreams and hard falls. Perhaps the height of their hubris came in 2019, when German financier Lars Windhorst arrived on the scene promising to turn Hertha into a 'big city club'. After four years and almost 400 million euros of investment, they were duly relegated in 2023.

For a long time, Union seemed even less likely to deliver on-field success. By the mid-2000s, years of financial trouble had pushed the club to the brink of disaster, and they were forced to rely on their own fans to bail them out. In 2004, Union supporters literally gave their own blood to save the club from bankruptcy, organising mass blood donations at a local clinic and donating the compensation fee to club coffers. Five years later, with the Alte Försterei under threat of demolition, they volunteered in their thousands to help renovate the stadium. While Hertha were dreaming big, Union were holed up in their south-eastern forest, scrapping like mad just to stay alive. Forner quotes a line from an East German youth propaganda song written by Bertolt Brecht: 'We had to look after ourselves.'

Yet conversely, it was the extent of the hardship that also laid the groundwork for Union's rapid rise. As the club stabilised in the third and second divisions, the stories of blood donations and fan-built stadiums began to attract new fans to Köpenick. Some were returnees, lapsed Union fans who were now rediscovering something of the old spirit. Others were newcomers from West Berlin, other cities or even abroad, who saw in Union a different, more community-led model of professional football. 'Our USP was always that we are a social club,' says Forner. 'That's what made us different: at Union, you always feel like you can get involved and make something happen.'

As more and more people flocked to the Alte Försterei, Union's prospects began to change. In 2011, they won a sensational derby victory over Hertha at the Olympiastadion, cementing their status as the city's second-biggest club. In 2017, they came within a whisker of promotion to the Bundesliga, and two years after that, they finally got there, beating Stuttgart on away goals in the promotion play-off.

'That moment,' says Forner, 'was the equivalent of the feeling I had when I first walked over the open border from East to West.' The difference was that this time it lasted. While the euphoria of 1989 had quickly given way to the tougher realities

Berliners from both East and West celebrate the fall of the Wall at the Brandenburg Gate in 1989. © imageBROKER.com/Norbert Michalke

of reunification, Union's fairytale just kept going. Two years after promotion, Union finished seventh and qualified for the Conference League, reaching Europe via the league for the first time in their history. A year later, they went one better and qualified for the Europa League, where they celebrated a historic second-round victory against Dutch giants Ajax. Just six months or so after that, they found themselves playing Real Madrid in the Champions League. Suddenly, the capital didn't have just one top-flight club with European aspirations, but two.

Between 2019 and 2023, Union went from 20,000 to 60,000 members, overtaking Hertha as the biggest club in the city. The growth was so rapid that they quickly outgrew their beloved Alte Försterei and were forced to play their Champions League games in the Olympiastadion to cope with demand. 'That was bitter for Hertha, and I can understand why a lot of them hate us now,' says Forner. 'Other clubs like Tennis Borussia and Blau-Weiß had come up to the Bundesliga before, but Hertha had always been by far the biggest club in the city. Then we came along and blew that to smithereens.'

In a city still marked by decades of division, there is arguably more than enough space for both clubs. Union, for their part, are a very East German success story. When they were promoted to the Bundesliga in 2019, they were the first club from the former GDR Oberliga to reach the top flight in a decade, bucking the trend of decline in the former East. As a community club owned a hundred per cent by its members, they also proved that you don't need to be RB Leipzig to have footballing success in the region. Hertha, meanwhile, have also returned to their roots in recent years, voting in Kay Bernstein, a former ultra, as president in 2022 and quickly cutting ties with the ill-fated investor Windhorst. Bernstein's sudden death in January 2024 shocked the club, but even in a year and a half, he had already set Hertha on a radical new course. Rather than dreaming big and trying to conquer the whole city, the club are now focused on youth development and rebuilding trust with their loyal core fanbase, most of which is still based in the former West Berlin.

In many ways, there is also now a healthier relationship between the two sides of the city than at any time in the last thirty years. Rather than one western giant in a constant state of overstretch, the capital now has two medium-to-large-sized clubs, both of whom are able to appeal to a slightly different constituency. The growing rivalry between the two teams has only galvanised their respective fanbases, and even after Hertha's relegation in 2023, Berlin's standing as a football city was still far higher than it had been for decades. In the late 2000s and 2010s, you were more likely to see Bayern shirts in a Berlin airport than those of Hertha or Union. In the autumn of 2023, clips of Union's Champions League games were playing above racks of replica shirts in the duty-free section.

That, in turn, is part of a wider process of normalisation in the city. After a century of turmoil and destruction, Berlin can now look back on thirty years of steady economic growth, and it is beginning to take on the characteristics of a normal capital. Union's rise has also coincided with a huge increase in wealth and prosperity in the east of the city. First, it was inner-city areas like Prenzlauer Berg and Friedrichshain that became affluent. Now, in the 2020s, the suburban east is also going through a population boom. Where previously, the former East lagged behind the more affluent West, now both sides of the city are flourishing and a new Berlin is emerging, which is more polished, wealthier and quite literally fatter. The rapidly expanding area around the city limits is known in Berlin slang as the *Speckgürtel*, or 'bacon belt'.

Progress, though, always involves loss. In both football and the city at large, there is also unease about what happens when you become too comfortable, too successful. 'We Union fans used to be proud of the fact that we supported a team with no hope of ever winning anything. Now the players have gone and ruined that for us,' cackles Forner. As many new fans stream in, older Unioners are left wondering how much of their original identity remains, whether their community ethos can survive the success it has created. When Union first pushed for promotion in 2017, fans had held up a banner reading 'Shit! We're going up!' It was a joke, but one that evoked real concerns about how success might change the club.

That is a common concern in modern Berlin. Over the last two decades, more and more money has flooded into the capital.

Average rents doubled between 2009 and 2023, and many of the iconic empty spaces, cultural venues and neighbourhoods have now fallen victim to rapid urban development. As neighbourhoods have gentrified and a once wide-open city has become increasingly claustrophobic, many wonder whether Berlin is losing something essential. Whether in the pursuit of growth and profit, it is sacrificing the very thing that made it unique in the first place.

Forner knows the city better than anyone. He admits that the areas in which he sells papers have indeed changed dramatically. 'The demographics are totally different in the pubs, it's become a lot more international, and we are also a tourist town these days,' he says, sounding almost as if he doesn't quite believe it. But he insists it would be wrong to resist the transformation. He notes that the GDR did not renew its economy, housing and ideas, and it eventually collapsed under the weight of its own stagnation. 'The only way a city develops is through change. The worst thing you can do is stand still and become calcified,' he says. 'Union have been successful because they have stayed true to themselves but not been scared of change.'

In a football culture like Germany's, fear of change is par for the course. Over the last two or three decades, German fans have fought tooth and nail to protect what they have and avoid the kind of rampant commercialism that has transformed the game elsewhere. But you cannot preserve everything in aspic, and even the most romantic football traditionalists must at some point move with the times. Change is not always a bad thing. As another, entirely different Berlin club are now showing, it can sometimes be long overdue.

At the *Park am Gleisdreieck* in the centre of Berlin, there are train tracks which run through the bushes. The word *Gleisdreieck* means 'track-triangle', and this was once the spot where Berlin's most important intercity railway lines converged on the central stations of Potsdamer Bahnhof and Anhalter Bahnhof. Both stations sustained heavy damage in the war, and were subsequently demolished, leaving the area to become one of many urban wastelands which backed up against the Wall. Only in the last decade or so has it come to life once again. While the U-Bahn trains rumble on elevated tracks overhead, the park below is a hive of activity, complete with beach volleyball courts, an outdoor gym and several beer gardens. Around the edges, shiny modern apartment buildings have shot up like daisies, creating a whole new neighbourhood just south of Potsdamer Platz. This is the new Berlin, a city of constant growth, where the scars of the old world are slowly receding into the undergrowth.

'They're going to build skyscrapers here soon. I'm not sure how much longer we have,' says Katharina Kurz, looking out the window from inside her restaurant. Even her business has only been there for a decade or so, but the pace of change is rapid in areas like these, and Kurz and her colleagues may soon have to make way for the latest grand construction project.

Kurz is the co-founder and managing director of BRLO, one of Germany's most successful craft beer breweries. Founded in 2014, its name comes from the old Slavic word for Berlin, but the company itself is very much a product of the new city. Its flagship brewery at Gleisdreieck is housed in a building made of thirty-eight 'upcycled' shipping containers and includes an on-site restaurant and beer garden. The entire complex, including the wooden beer benches, is painted in black and white, and the menu offers more than a dozen different beers with names like 'Office Legend' and 'OK Czech!' It is all a far cry from Berlin's traditional *Eckkneipen*, or corner pubs, where the air is thick with smoke and there is usually a choice of two mass-produced pilseners. But then that is also the point: 'We are very proud of our beer culture here in Germany, but in truth it is quite conservative,' says Kurz. 'Why does beer always have to be pilsener? Why does pub food always have to be schnitzel and sausages? At BRLO, we are trying to shake things up a bit.'

In the 1980s and 1990s, it was the artists and anarchists who were on the cutting edge in Berlin. Nowadays, it is the restaurateurs and entrepreneurs who are changing the city. Over the last two decades, Berlin has developed a reputation as the start-up capital of Europe, and BRLO is just one of the countless ventures that have thrived in the capital, from tech firms and online retailers to NGOs and universities. Often, they are founded not by Berliners, but by people like Kurz, who have moved to the city from abroad or elsewhere in Germany and have found space in Berlin to shake up old certainties and try something new. Kurz, who is originally from Fürth in northern Bavaria, is not just doing that with beer. She is also doing it with football.

In the summer of 2022, she and a group of fellow entrepreneurs announced a new project which they said would mark a 'revolution in football'. The all-female team, which included former Germany international Ariane Hingst and business guru Verena Pausder, had pooled resources to take over the women's team of FC Viktoria Berlin, a semi-professional club from the southern district of Lichterfelde. Their aim was not just to establish a new force in Berlin football, but to transform the women's game entirely. 'Our aim is to reach the women's Bundesliga within five years, and in doing so to get more visibility, more equal pay and recognition for women's football,' Kurz and her colleagues announced in the press release.

Germany had once been the dominant power of European women's football, winning eight European Championships and two World Cup titles in the 1990s and 2000s. But when they lost the final of the 2022 Women's European Championship to England at Wembley a few weeks after the Viktoria announcement, it seemed like a symbolic changing of the guard. While the women's game was going from strength to strength in countries like England, in Germany there were fears it was stagnating. The national team had long since surrendered its supremacy, while the once dominant club teams like Wolfsburg, 1. FFC Frankfurt and Turbine Potsdam had not won a Champions League title since 2015. With their new venture in Berlin, Kurz and her co-founders wanted to shake German football out of its stupor.

'It had always annoyed me how women's football was treated,' says Kurz, noting that her own love of the game was cut short by a lack of facilities, even at a time when Germany were still world leaders. 'I played football until I was twelve, but after that, girls weren't allowed to play in the boys' teams, and there was no girls' team in the whole of Fürth. So I just stopped playing.' Like many others, she also felt that women's football was under-served by a conservative broadcast media, wasting immense potential to draw in new audiences. And she had proof. In 2019, BRLO became one of the first beer gardens in Germany to show live broadcasts of Women's World Cup games. Initially, Kurz feared that she would lose money on the idea. In reality, they were booked out for almost every game.

At Viktoria, she and her colleagues aimed to apply the same hands-on attitude on a much larger scale. 'Rather than moaning about what wasn't being done in women's football, we wanted to just start doing things,' says Kurz. Their model was Angel City FC, the women's club franchise founded by Natalie Portman and Serena Williams in Los Angeles two years earlier. And while Viktoria didn't quite have the same Hollywood firepower, they did prove to be a remarkably successful publicity machine. Within months of the initial announcement, German celebrities like the tennis legend Steffi Graf and comedian Carolin Kebekus were among the dozens of people who had signed up as ambassadors and co-investors. The little stadium in Lichterfelde was suddenly attracting crowds of up to two thousand for regional league women's games, numbers that would have been unthinkable just months before.

Berlin, after all, was hardly a stronghold of women's football in 2022. 1. FFC Turbine, from neighbouring Potsdam, had once been the biggest women's team in the country but had since fallen on hard times. Hertha didn't even have a women's team, while Union's was still part of the amateur set-up. Only Türkiyemspor in Kreuzberg were punching above their weight when it came to investment in the women's game, and as a perennially cash-strapped lower-league team, their power was limited. Once Viktoria arrived, that began to change. In the autumn of 2022, Hertha announced a 'reset in our women's and girls' football', and took steps to expand their women's section. In the summer of 2023, Union declared they were professionalising their women's team, which already played alongside Viktoria in the regional league. 'They probably would have ended up doing that anyway, but I think we did give the big clubs a kick up the backside,' says Kurz.

Perhaps inevitably, there was also a backlash. 'Investor' is a dirty word for many German football fans, and Viktoria's investor-driven model was bound to rub some people the wrong way. Kurz and her fellow founders had also taken over direct control of the women's team, repackaging it as a limited company within the structure of the overall club, which led some to question whether the entire project was really in the spirit of 50+1 and member-run clubs. The editor of *11 Freunde*, one of Germany's biggest football magazines, referred to it rather archly as 'a construct that will take some getting used to', while others compared Viktoria to RB Leipzig. Kurz rolls her eyes at the notion. 'The comparison with RB always makes me laugh, because we are talking about a totally different starting point,' she says. Red Bull is a global brand which has unilateral control over RB, she points out. Viktoria's investors, by contrast, are all private individuals, and can only invest up to 50,000 euros per person.

At the same time, she admits that Viktoria are quite happy to be stirring things up a bit. 'We use the word "investor" deliberately, because we want to show people that women's sport does actually need some money if it is going to succeed. Otherwise you'll never improve the structures and nothing will change. You need attention, you need cash. Of course we want to avoid the kind of financial madness we see in the men's game, but we are a long way away from that at the moment. What we should really be talking about is why women can't make a decent living playing football.'

You get the feeling that Kurz has faced her fair share of mansplaining. This is a woman who founded a brewery in Germany, and as she notes at one point with an enormous grin: 'The German beer industry is a sausage fest.' Football, too, is hardly a haven of gender equality at the best of times, and Kurz spies a latent misogyny in the criticism of Viktoria. 'It's as if with the men, everyone just expects them to be evil capitalists and you can't do anything about it. But as soon as women start investing money, people start to say: "Oh, not you too!"'

There is, perhaps, an even deeper issue at play here. Who owns German football culture? Who gets to decide what is right and wrong? In the case of Viktoria, a lot of people in German football slipped into their usual positions: pro-investment, anti-investment, tradition or commercialism. Yet not all investment is automatically bad, and not all traditions are born equal. German fans may be the most empowered in the world, but they are also largely male, largely white, largely heterosexual. As Kurz points out: when people talk about German football culture, they don't tend to include women's football.

Viktoria, she argues, are building a new fan culture. Though the women's team play in the same stadium as the men's, the atmosphere at their games is much less aggressive, much more accessible. That in turn is drawing new people into the game, who may otherwise feel alienated by the stricter, more conservative

The all-female founders of FC Viktoria, including former Germany international Ariane Hingst (third from right) and craft beer brewer Katharina Kurz (top right). © FC Viktoria Berlin

confines of men's football. While the men obsess over tradition, the women are by definition creating something for future generations. 'My son is two years old, and he's only ever been to Viktoria. I don't think he even knows that men can play football,' says Kurz.

As with any revolution, there are always winners and losers. Even within women's football, there are those who mourn for what is being lost. Viktoria's success is also part of a trend which has seen the women's Bundesliga lose some of its individuality. As more and more professional men's clubs invest in their women's teams, some of the women-only clubs which were once the driving force behind women's football in Germany have struggled to keep up. Turbine Potsdam, six-time German champions and six-time East German champions, were relegated from the Bundesliga in 2023. Four-time Women's Champions League winners 1. FFC Frankfurt were subsumed into Eintracht Frankfurt in 2020.

Yet it is a bit like with Berlin: you can't stop the train once it begins to roll. A craft beer company like BRLO is arguably a symptom of the city's gentrification, part of the same process which pushes rents up and begins to close off the wild spaces which used to make the city exciting and different. But like Forner, Kurz argues that it is madness to try and stop the wheel from turning. 'It's a shame that the city is losing these wilder, rougher spots. But you can't just preserve the status quo: and I do think that Berlin is going through a good development,' she says.

Whether or not the project will last is another matter. Viktoria are extremely well marketed, but that does not necessarily mean their initiative will bear fruit. For every BRLO in Berlin, there are also countless start-ups that have crashed, burned or quietly sidled off the stage with a whimper. Viktoria missed out on promotion in 2023, and the jury is still out on whether they can really revolutionise women's football in Germany. There have, after all, been false dawns before. When Germany hosted the 2011 Women's World Cup, there was optimism that it would prompt a new era of mainstream popularity and investment. Instead, Germany failed to develop its women's game as quickly as other countries did over the following decade.

But Kurz thinks it is different this time. She argues that the success of Viktoria shows that something is changing in German society. 'I just think the time is ripe on so many levels. A lot of things have come together in the last few years, from the #MeToo movement to new alliances between female business leaders,' she says. 'The issue of gender equality is so much more present now than it was in 2011. And I hope that means we have a momentum behind us which cannot be stopped.'

At Bayern Munich, there is a banner which the ultras hang behind the goal during home games which reads: *Gegen den modernen Fußball.* 'Against modern football.' It is a simple message, and one which many German fans – however much they hate Bayern – can get firmly behind. Germany is a place where many people reject the financial excesses of the modern game, and a place where many others come to find a football they have lost elsewhere.

Yet perhaps the point is not simply to fight modern football, but also to change it. In Berlin, clubs like Union and Viktoria are building new visions of the modern game. And perhaps it is no surprise that they are doing so from the German capital. In Berlin, you can't stop change. The only option is to try and shape it.

For all Berlin is changing and normalising, it is still a very different kind of capital. The rivalry between Hertha and Union may have breathed new life into the city's football, but they remain oddball clubs in an oddball capital, still far away from challenging the likes of Bayern, Dortmund, Leipzig and Leverkusen. In a country like Germany, where regionalism is so important and power has always been spread between the major cities, there can never be one single centre of gravity. Berlin may be the seat of political power, but the biggest companies, the biggest airports, the biggest banks and the biggest football clubs are all elsewhere in the country.

Likewise, German football still plays by different rules to the other major powers of European football and it too is a product of the country's history. The hegemony of club football over the national team reflects a country where regionalism rules supreme and patriotism is difficult, while the scars of the division between East and West are still tangible in the landscape of the Bundesliga. The enduring wider ideological divides in German society have also played out on the terraces, as a new era of commercialism and growth has brought football crashing into the mainstream, and a new wave of organised fan culture has grown to meet it. The Bundesliga's tightrope act between commercialism and tradition reflects a country where consensus is king, but also one where grassroots activism and community organisation are ingrained in many people.

So where is that country headed now, in the mid-2020s? Olaf Scholz's Zeitenwende speech in 2022 was primarily about defence and security, about Germany's place in the world and its responsibility to NATO and EU allies. But talk of a new era and a turning point in history also touched a nerve in society at large. When

Germany last hosted a major football tournament, things were different. The 2006 World Cup was arguably the zenith of post-reunification German optimism and the high point of a thirty-year golden age. This time around, the country is in a different place, more tentative about the future and more divided over its present.

In the summer of 2024, new challenges abounded. Germany's juggernaut economy slipped into recession in 2023, prompting fears of a greater decline. In Frankfurt, the European Central Bank spent the same year battling to control spiralling inflation. In the north, where the Russian gas pipelines have been shut off and the Port of Hamburg has opened up to Chinese investment, Germany is re-evaluating its place in the global marketplace. In Bavaria and Stuttgart, the success of 'Made in Germany' is wobbling as the car industry faces new challenges of international competition and the green transition. Politically too, the atmosphere is heating up. In western regions like the Ruhr and the Rhineland, climate change has begun to make itself felt, with devastating floods in 2021 having a major effect on the outcome of that year's elections. In eastern cities like Leipzig, the debate over reunification and east–west relations rages on. In Berlin, politics is becoming ever more polarised: 2024 began with mass strikes and large-scale protests over the government's agricultural policies.

There are also reasons for optimism. Germany is a resilient country. It built a functioning democracy from the ashes of Nazism and overcame forty years of Cold War division to emerge as a unified whole. Since reunification, it has bounced back from several recessions to retain its status as the fourth-largest economy in the world. For much of its post-war history, this is a country that has looked crises squarely in the face and come out all the stronger for it. Yet if the history of the country and its capital tell us one thing, it is that Germany is a project that is, by definition, never finished. As former Chancellor and one-time Berlin mayor Willy Brandt put it in 1992: 'Nothing comes from itself and very little lasts. Every time demands its own answers.'

Football provides a snapshot of Germany in its current time. A country that is forever defined by its own history, but now stands once again on the cusp of something new. In Germany, you can never escape the past. But each time demands its own answers, and each future will be different. Both on and off the pitch.

EPILOGUE

EURO
APRIL 2024

Three months before the start of Euro 2024, Julian Nagelsmann sat in the DFB headquarters in Frankfurt and confessed to a room full of Germany fans that he was a bad loser.

'I always want to win. As a kid, I used to argue with my mother when we played board games. She'd tell me I should learn how to lose, but I don't see it that way. Sometimes you have to accept defeat, but you should never learn how to lose. Why should you learn how to do that? Losing is shit.'

It was vintage Nagelsmann: the kind of controlled Bavarian bravado that had propelled him throughout his rollercoaster career. This was the man who had taken his first Bundesliga job at the age of twenty-eight, becoming the league's youngest ever first team coach. By the time he hit thirty-four, he had won the league with Bayern Munich. And now, here he was: in charge of the national team and on a mission to restore the famous German winning mentality.

Until that point, the mood in the host nation had been bleak. The national team had not reached the quarter-finals of a major competition in almost a decade, and had lost six of eleven games the previous year. The country at large was also in a crisis of confidence ahead of the Euros. After a winter of air and rail strikes, there were fears that Germany was ill-equipped to deal with the influx of twelve million visiting football fans. Amid deepening political divisions and intense soul-searching over the conflicts in Ukraine and Gaza, there seemed little hope that even football could bring the nation together.

Yet as spring arrived, things started to look a little rosier. In March, Nagelsmann moved to revive the German team with some bold selection decisions and was rewarded with victories over France and the Netherlands. In club football, meanwhile, there were signs that 2024 could yet prove a historic year for the German game.

In April, Bayer Leverkusen rampaged to their first ever Bundesliga title, ending Bayern's toxic decade of dominance and breaking countless records along the way. As their fans stormed the pitch and the players drenched coach Xabi Alonso in copious litres of beer, it seemed a reminder that football still had the power to surprise. A week later, Leverkusen cruised through the quarter-finals of the Europa League, while both Bayern and Dortmund battled their way into the last four of the Champions League. For the first time since 1995, Germany had three teams in the semi-finals of European competition. The national game was back, with at least a hint of its old swagger.

Was this the Euros effect? The fabled power of a major tournament to heal a country and launch a new golden era? A repeat of the magical moment of 2006 and the start of a new summer fairytale? Perhaps. But Germany is not a monolith and football rarely offers only one narrative. In reality, both the country and its football culture are far too complex and conflicted to simply live happily ever after.

For a start, success is not the only yardstick. For all Nagelsmann's well-timed populism, there were plenty of signs in 2024 that German fans care about more than just winning. In January and February, the Bundesliga was rocked by fan protests after the league announced plans to create a new media subsidiary and sell a stake of it to private equity investors. For weeks on end, protesting fans deliberately disrupted games across the country, throwing tennis balls and other items onto the pitch and bringing several matches to the brink of cancellation. To an outsider, it seemed an arcane dispute, but for German fans it was fundamental. Aggrieved by a lack of transparency and consultation, they cast the issue as a battle for the very survival of fan democracy.

When the investment plans were abandoned in mid-February, it was arguably a far more significant victory than any triumph on the pitch. Rather than a single, symbolic demonstration, fan groups had coordinated across the country, garnered widespread public support and refused to back down until their demands were met. They had forced the league's hand in one of the most dramatic and effective displays of fan power in the history of European football. For good or ill, it seemed like a defining moment. A crucial battle in the ongoing conflict between football as a competitive, commercialised sport and football as a cultural good.

That battle was also being fought elsewhere. The bitter internal power struggles at clubs like Stuttgart, Schalke and 1860 Munich raged on in the 2023/24 season, while away fans continued to protest at RB Leipzig. Even Leverkusen's title win – arguably the best thing to happen to the Bundesliga in years – spoke of the conflicts within the German game. Though many were thrilled to see Bayern knocked off their perch, there was also a bitter note for the game's traditionalists. Leverkusen are the club of the local pharmaceuticals giant Bayer, an unloved side from a small, industrial town just outside Cologne. In many ways, they were the league's first ever "plastic club", and they are still one of only two that have an exception to the 50+1 rule. When Leverkusen win, it is quite literally a win for big business. And for many, that means a defeat for fan culture, tradition and romance.

Leverkusen fans would see it differently of course. But the point is that for many in Germany, the soul of the game is always the primary concern. For them, football is less about bragging rights or petty rivalries and more about cultural conservation. That might mean helping to preserve the local dialect in a place like Cologne or maintaining the memory of a bygone age in the Ruhr and the East. In Munich, the game might express a haughty Bavarian exceptionalism. In Hamburg, it might stand for a set of political convictions. To reduce the game to a simple question of victory or defeat would, in any case, be to miss the point entirely.

Likewise, Germany's hopes and fears ahead of Euro 2024 are also about more than just football. As the country gears up to host the tournament in the spring, many are already more concerned with the wider legacy than they are with the fate of the national team. As well as fretting about infrastructure and security, that also means asking how the tournament would change society. 'In Germany and Europe, the feeling of social cohesion has suffered a lot lately. I want to make it clear to people that we can use this tournament to bring society together,' tournament director Philipp Lahm told a police conference in Berlin in April.

Yet if Germany learned anything from its first summer fairytale, it is that football is not a panacea. In 2006, as the national team rode a wave of national optimism, it was easy to conclude that the World Cup was reshaping society. Yet as society's divisions deepened in the 2010s, football was powerless to stop the rot. Just as other nations in Europe have discovered in recent decades, football's power to truly unite a country – or even a continent – is ultimately limited.

What it can do is hold up a mirror. The passions and neuroses of German football run far deeper than the game itself, and they offer a warts-and-all window into the soul of an often-misunderstood country. If there is any lasting legacy from Euro 2024, then perhaps it will be that thousands of football fans had the chance to look more closely at Germany and move beyond the clichés and preconceptions. And that, in the end, may be worth as much as any trophy.

ACKNOWLEDGEMENTS

First and foremost, *Played in Germany* would not exist without the help of my wife, Josie, who came up with the title and is the greatest travel companion, editor and ally that anyone could wish for.

The book would also be nothing without its interviewees, all of whom were very gracious in giving up their time and effort to help me. Special thanks to André Göhre, Olivier Kruschinski, Annette Kritzler and Stephanie Dilba, who welcomed me onto invaluable guided tours in Leipzig, Dortmund, Gelsenkirchen and Munich.

Research and reporting would have been significantly harder without the generous help of friends and colleagues like Archie Rhind-Tutt, Charlotte Bruch, Stefan Hermanns, Karsten Kellermann, Jonny Walsh and in particular Tom Julian, who went above and beyond to support me in his role at DFL Deutsche Fußball Liga.

Thanks to Steffen Mayr-Uhlmann, Tina Niedecken, Jens Volke, Sven Brux, Max Geis and Matze Koch for their help in arranging interviews and sourcing photos, as well as to the press offices of FC Bayern, FC St. Pauli, Borussia Dortmund, Borussia Mönchengladbach, Chemie Leipzig, Mercedes-Benz Classic and Bündnis90/Die Grünen.

I am immensely grateful to my agent, Robert Dudley, and my publisher, Duckworth, for helping me make the project a reality, especially in such a short timeframe. Special thanks to my editor, Rob Wilding, for his tireless hard work, his infectious enthusiasm and his expert guidance from start to finish. Thank you also to Deborah Blake and Alice Brett for the copy edit, to Luke Bird for another wonderful cover, and to everyone who has helped with production and promotion.

I am indebted to my friends Jack, Harry, Katie and Otis for their marvellous company on trips to Düsseldorf, Cologne and Munich, and to my family for their constant love and support. Finally and always, thanks to my dad, Jim, for the joy of football and writing.

LIST OF ILLUSTRATIONS

p. 4: Union Berlin fans protest against Red Bull in Leipzig in 2020. © Matthias Koch

p. 20: A statue of Faust and Mephistopheles outside the Auerbachs Keller in Leipzig. © Kit Holden

p. 33: Hennes IX, Köln's famous goat mascot, with his minder Ingo Reipka in 2023. © 1. FC Köln

p. 38: The Kölner Dom. © Kit Holden

p. 52: The site of Borussia Monchengladbach's famous Bökelberg-Stadion, now a housing estate. © Kit Holden

p. 63: The stained-glass window of St. Aloysius at St. Joseph's Church, Gelsenkirchen. © Olivier Kruschinski

p. 75: Borussia Dortmund players celebrate with fans at Borsigplatz in 2017. © Borussia Dortmund

p. 82: The "Yellow Wall", Signal Iduna Park. © Borussia Dortmund

p. 92: Gottlieb Daimler in his 1886 "motor-carriage". © Mercedes Benz Classic

p. 108: The Porsche logo. © 2023 Dr. Ing. h.c. F. Porsche AG

p. 115: A depiction of the first ever national parliament convened in the Paulskirche, Frankfurt. © Historisches Museum Frankfurt C12527

p. 139: Omid Nouripour in the Waldstadion. © Victor Martini / Bündnis90 Die Grünen
p. 147: St. Pauli's Millerntor stadium. © FCSP
p. 151: Residents clear the barricades on Hafenstraße, Hamburg, in 1987. © dpa picture alliance/Alamy Stock Photo
p. 161: The Port of Hamburg. © Kit Holden
p. 172: Manuel Neuer, Harry Kane and Jamal Musiala at Oktoberfest in 2023. © FC Bayern München
p. 185: The scoreboard at the Grünwalder Stadion. © Matthias Koch

ENDNOTES

1. 19.1 per cent in 1998, 18.7 per cent in 1999. Data: Bundesagentur für Arbeit, 'Registrierte Arbeitslose, Arbeitslosenquote nach Gebietsstand', Statistisches Bundesamt (Destatis), 2023.
2. Data: Baghdady, Anne/Würz, Markus, 'Leben in Trümmern', Lebendiges Museum Online, Stiftung Haus der Geschichte der Bundesrepublik Deutschland, 2024.
3. 14.1 per cent in 2022, average of 15.5 per cent between 2001 and 2022 compared to national average 8.4 per cent. Data: Bundesagentur für Arbeit/Statistische Ämter des Bundes und der Länder, 'Die 25 kreisfreien Städte und Landkreise mit der höchsten Arbeitslosenquote in Deutschland im Jahr 2022', Statista, 2023.
4. Data: Schührer, Susanne, 'Türkeistämmige Personen in Deutschland: Erkenntnisse aus der Repräsentativuntersuchung "Ausgewählte Migrantengruppen in Deutschland 2015" (RAM)', Bundesamt für Migration und Flüchtlinge, 2018.
5. Data: 'Automobilindustrie', Bundesministerium für Wirtschaft und Klimaschutz, 2024.
6. Data: 'Liste der aktiven Interessenvertreter/-innen nach Höhe der finanziellen Aufwendungen (absteigend)', Lobbyregister im Deutschen Bundestag, 2024.
7. Data: United States Holocaust Museum, 'Estimated number of victims of the Holocaust and Nazi crimes against humanity during the Second World War from 1933 to 1945, by background, *Statista*, 2020.
8. Data: Bundeskriminalamt/Bundesministerium des Innern/Bundesamt für Verfassungsschutz, 'Anzahl der politisch motivierten Straftaten und Gewalttaten mit rechtsextremistischem Hintergrund in Deutschland von 2010 bis 2022', *Statista*, 2023.
9. Data: 'Seegüterumschlag, 1989 bis 2022, in Millionen Tonnen', Port of Hamburg, 2023.

10 Data: Statistische Ämter des Bundes und der Länder, 'Bruttoinlandsprodukt, Bruttowertschöpfung in den kreisfreien Städten und Landkreisen der Bundesrepublik Deutschland 1992 und 1994 bis 2021, Statistikportal, 2023.

BIBLIOGRAPHY

Print

Biermann, Christoph, *Wenn wir vom Fußball träumen* (Kiepenheuer & Witsch, 2014)
Dilba, Stephanie, *TSV 1860 München Fußballfibel* (Culturcon Medien, 2019)
Formeseyn, Axel, *Unser HSV* (Edition Temmen, 2008)
Fuge, Jens, *Chemisches Element: Meine 45 Jahre in Leutzsch* (Backroad Diaries, 2021)
Fulbrook, Mary, *The People's State: East German Society from Hitler to Honecker* (Yale University Press, 2005)
Hawes, James, *The Shortest History of Germany* (Old Street Publishing, 2017)
Hering, Hartmut (ed.), *Im Land der tausend Derbys: Die Fußball-Geschichte des Ruhrgebiets* (Verlag Die Werkstatt, 2002)
Hesse, Uli, *Tor! The Story of German Football* (WSC Books, 2002)
Hirschmann, Jens P., *Festschrift: 125 Jahre VfB Leipzig* (1. FC Lokomotive Leipzig/Schriftwerk GmbH, 2018)
Holden, Kit, *Scheisse! We're Going Up! The Unexpected Rise of Berlin's Rebel Football Club* (Duckworth, 2022)
Hoyer, Katja, *Beyond the Wall: East Germany, 1949–1990* (Allen Lane, 2023)
Koch, Matthias, *'Immer weiter, ganz nach vorn': Die Geschichte des 1. FC Union Berlin* (Verlag Die Werkstatt, 2013)
Leischwitz, Christoph, *Mia san die Bayern! Die Geschichte der rot-weißen Fankultur* (Verlag Die Werkstatt, 2020)
MacGregor, Neil, *Germany: Memories of a Nation* (Allen Lane, 2014)
Peiffer, Lorenz and Schulze-Marmeling, Dietrich (eds), *Hakenkreuz und rundes Leder: Fußball im Nationalsozialismus* (Verlag Die Werkstatt, 2008)
Schulze-Marmeling, Dietrich (ed.), *Davidstern und Lederball: Die Geschichte der Juden im deutschen und internationalen Fußball* (Verlag Die Werkstatt, 2003)
Thoma, Matthias, *Wir waren die Juddebube: Eintracht Frankfurt in der NS-Zeit* (Verlag Die Werkstatt, 2007)

Udelhoven, Dirk, *111 Gründe, den 1. FC Köln zu lieben* (Schwartzkopf & Schwartzkopf, 2016)
Willmann, Frank (ed.), *Stadionpartisanen: Fans und Hooligans in der DDR* (Neues Leben, 2007)

Online

'Bergarbeit und Zwangsarbeit im Ruhrgebiet', *Arbeitskreis der NS-Gedenkstätten und Erinnerungsorte in NRW*, 2010, https://www.ns-gedenkstaetten.de/arbeitskreis/aktuelles/detailseite/bergarbeit-und-zwangsarbeit-im-ruhrgebiet (accessed 16 February 2024)

Brost, Marc, Fritsch, Oliver and Storn, Arne, 'House of Stuttgarts', *Zeit Online*, 2021, https://www.zeit.de/serie/house-of-stuttgarts (accessed 16 February 2024)

'Bunker Feldstraße: Buntes Treiben hinter grauen Mauern', *Hamburg.de*, https://www.hamburg.de/sehenswuerdigkeiten-erlebnis/10445612/bunker-feldstrasse/ (accessed 16 February 2024)

'Das sind die größten Arbeitgeber in Stuttgart', *Stuttgarter Zeitung*, 2019, https://www.stuttgarter-zeitung.de/inhalt.entwicklung-der-beschaeftigung-das-sind-die-groessten-arbeitgeber-in-stuttgart.6258956f-b1f9-472d-82f3-bc7713b631b6.html (accessed 16 February 2024)

'Der Kampf um die Hafenstraße in der Chronologie', *NDR*, 2022, https://www.ndr.de/geschichte/schauplaetze/Hafenstrasse-Hamburg-Chronologie-eines-Kampfes,hafenstrasse153.html (accessed 16 February 2024)

'Die Geschichte des Oktoberfests: Historischer Streifzug durch die Wiesn-Historie', *Oktoberfest.de*, https://www.oktoberfest.de/magazin/tradition/die-geschichte-des-oktoberfests (accessed 16 February 2024)

'Diesen Plan hat Campino mit Jürgen Klopp bei Fortuna', *Rheinische Post*, 2023, https://rp-online.de/sport/fussball/fortuna/fortuna-duesseldorf-was-campino-von-toten-hosen-mit-juergen-klopp-vor-hat-nach-seiner-zeit-beim-fc-liverpool_aid-91368153 (accessed 16 February 2024)

Franz, Corinna, 'Umgang mit der NS-Vergangenheit', *Konrad-adenauer.de*, https://www.konrad-adenauer.de/politikfelder/seite/umgang-mit-der-ns-vergangenheit/ (accessed 16 February 2024)

'Fritz Walter zum 100.: Der "Held von Bern" unvergessen', *Süddeutsche Zeitung*, 2020, https://www.sueddeutsche.de/sport/fussball-fritz-walter-zum-100-der-held-von-bern-unvergessen-dpa.urn-newsml-dpa-com-20090101-201030-99-143331 (accessed 16 February 2024)

'Geschichte des Areals Römerkastell', *MKM Römerkastell Stuttgart*, https://www.roemerkastell-stuttgart.com/geschichte/ (accessed 16 February 2024)

'Gründer und Wegbereiter: Gottlieb Daimler', *Mercedes-Benz Group*, https://group.mercedes-benz.com/unternehmen/tradition/gruender-wegbereiter/gottlieb-daimler.html (accessed 16 February 2024)

BIBLIOGRAPHY

'Hertha BSC gegen Union: So war das vor 25 Jahren', *Tagesspiegel*, 2015, https://www.tagesspiegel.de/sport/hertha-bsc-gegen-union-so-war-das-vor-25-jahren-1771342.html (accessed 16 February 2024)

Jordan, Markus, 'Wer war Gottlieb Daimler?', *MBpassion.de*, 2020, https://mbpassion.de/2022/06/wer-war-gottlieb-daimler/ (accessed 16 February 2024)

Kleinmann, Patrick, 'Cohn-Bendit: "Diese Mannschaft war ein Spiegelbild des Aufbruchs"', *Kicker*, 2022, https://www.kicker.de/cohn-bendit-diese-mannschaft-war-ein-spiegelbild-des-aufbruchs-905925/artikel (accessed 16 February 2024)

'Kölner Dom: Ein Jahrhundertprojekt und die vollkommende Kathedrale', *Katholisch.de*, 2020, https://www.katholisch.de/artikel/27293-koelner-dom-ein-jahrhundertprojekt-und-die-vollkommene-kathedrale (accessed 16 February 2024)

Kraushaar, Wolfgang, 'Denkmodelle der 68er', *Bundeszentrale für politische Bildung*, 2008, https://www.bpb.de/themen/zeit-kulturgeschichte/68er-bewegung/51820/denkmodelle-der-68er/ (accessed 16 February 2024)

Kronenberg, Volker, '"Verfassungspatriotimus" im vereinten Deutschland', *Bundeszentrale für politische Bildung*, 2009, https://www.bpb.de/shop/zeitschriften/apuz/31878/verfassungs-patriotismus-im-vereinten-deutschland/ (accessed 16 February 2024)

Löttel, Holger, 'Konrad Adenauer und Preußen', *Konrad-adenauer.de*, https://www.konrad-adenauer.de/politikfelder/seite/konrad-adenauer-und-preussen/ (accessed 16 February 2024)

'Mieten steigen ortsweise um 100 Prozent, Kaufpreise um 200 Prozent', *Tagesspiegel*, 2023, https://interaktiv.tagesspiegel.de/lab/mietsteigerungen-wohnungskrise-in-welchen-deutschen-staedten-die-mieten-und-kaufpreise-besonders-stark-steigen/ (accessed 16 February 2024)

Näher, Thomas, 'Der lange Blonde wird 70 Jahre alt', *Stuttgarter Nachrichten*, 2014 https://www.stuttgarter-nachrichten.de/inhalt.guenter-netzer-zum-geburtstag-der-lange-blonde-wird-70-jahrealt.7e53b289-d971-4a1a-9bf8-d7a9a7616051.html (accessed 16 February 2024)

'Revolution und Frankfurter Nationalversammlung 848/1849', *Deutscher Bundestag*, https://www.bundestag.de/parlament/geschichte/parlamentarismus/1848 (accessed 16 February 2024)

Ruf, Christoph, '"Wir würden selbst den Teufel mit offenen Armen empfangen"', *Spiegel Online*, 2009, https://www.spiegel.de/sport/fussball/red-bull-in-leipzig-wir-wuerden-selbst-den-teufel-mit-offenen-armen-empfangen-a-630820.html (accessed 16 February 2024)

Scholz, Olaf, 'Reden zur Zeitenwende', *Die Bundesregierung*, 2022, https://www.bundesregierung.de/resource/blob/992814/2131062/78d39dda6647d7f835bbe76713d30c31/bundeskanzler-olaf-scholz-reden-zur-zeitenwende-download-bpa-data.pdf (accessed 16 February 2024)

'Vor 30 Jahren: Die erste Montagsdemonstration', *Bundeszentrale für politische Bildung*, 2019, https://www.bpb.de/kurz-knapp/hintergrund-aktuell/295940/vor-30-jahren-die-erste-montagsdemonstration/ (accessed 16 February 2024)

'Vor 60 Jahren: "Ja" zur Bundesliga', *DFL*, 2022, https://www.dfl.de/de/aktuelles/vor-60-jahren-ja-zur-bundesliga/ (accessed 16 February 2024)

'Vor 65 Jahren: Bonn setzt sich gegen Frankfurt durch', *Deutscher Bundestag*, 2014, https://www.bundestag.de/webarchiv/textarchiv/2014/kw45_regierungssitz_bonn-337836 (accessed 16 February 2024)

'Vor 120 Jahren: Der DFB wird gegründet', *Deutscher Fußball-Bund*, 2020, https://www.dfb.de/news/detail/vor-120-jahren-der-dfb-wird-gegruendet-212342/ (accessed 16 February 2024)

'Werner Fassbender ist verstorben', Fortuna Düsseldorf, 2017, https://www.f95.de/aktuell/news/verein/detail/21378-werner-fassbender-ist-verstorben/ (accessed 16 February 2024)

Winters, Peter Jochen, 'Der Frankfurter Auschwitz-Prozess: Ein Rückblick 50 Jahre nach dem Urteil', *Bundeszentrale für politische Bildung*, 2015, https://www.bpb.de/shop/zeitschriften/apuz/204287/der-frankfurter-auschwitz-prozess/ (accessed 16 February 2024)

Wolfrum, Edgar, 'Geschichte der Erinnerungskultur in der DDR und BRD', *Bundeszentrale für politische Bildung*, 2008, https://www.bpb.de/themen/erinnerung/geschichte-und-erinnerung/39814/geschichte-der-erinnerungskultur-in-der-ddr-und-brd/ (accessed 16 February 2024)

'Zu Hennes Weiswilers 100.: "Ein Leben für den Fußball"', *Deutscher Fußball-Bund*, 2019, https://www.dfb.de/news/detail/zu-hennes-weiswilers-100-ein-leben-fuer-den-fussball-211067/ (accessed 16 February 2024)

Other sources

11 Freunde
11km - Der Fußball-Reiseblog
ARD
Bild
Deutsches Historisches Museum
Eintracht Frankfurt Museum
Frankfurter Allgemeine Zeitung
Historisches Museum Frankfurt
Hörfehler - Podcast zur Fußball-Zeitgeschichte
Kicker
Süddeutsche Zeitung
Tagesspiegel
ZDF
Zeitgeschichtliches Forum Leipzig

Kit Holden is a British-German author and journalist based in Berlin. He covers football for *Der Tagesspiegel* and AFP, and he has also written for *The Athletic*, *Guardian* and *Die Zeit*. His first book *Scheisse! We're Going Up!* was shortlisted for the 2023 *Sunday Times* Sports Book Awards.